A Victory For Miriam!

The Little Jewish Girl Who Defied The Nazis

Miriam M. Brysk & Joanne D. Gilbert

ADIRA PRESS

Las Vegas, Nevada 2019

In memory of the six million
Jewish men, women, and children
who were murdered in the Holocaust,
including our own beloved relatives:

Ita and *Avrom Zablocki, Chana Liba Miasnik,*
Ala Wilner, Tadek Wilner, Sarah Wineman,
Rivka Wineman, Malka Wineman

And in honor of Holocaust survivors,
including Miriam's parents:
Bronka and *Chaim Miasnik*
and her husband:
Henry Brysk

We dedicate this book to our children:
Havi Mandell, Judy Brysk, and *Greg Gilbert*
to our grandchildren:
Benjamin, Joshua, David, Sarah, Hannah, and *Julia*
and to Miriam's great-grandson:
Elian

"Look at how a single candle can both defy and define the darkness."

— Anne Frank

*"Holding our breaths. Waiting to be captured and shot at any moment.
But suddenly the silence returns. The Germans are gone, and we're alive.
Protected by the moonless night. We held on to live another day."*

— Miriam Brysk

PRAISE for: *A VICTORY FOR MIRIAM!*
The Little Jewish Girl Who Defied The Nazis

"*A VICTORY FOR MIRIAM! The Little Jewish Girl Who Defied the Nazis*
is a wonderful book."

As a teacher who conducts workshops for other teachers who plan to incorporate
the Holocaust in their courses, I have been fortunate to be able to use Joanne Gilbert's
engaging and inspiring first book, *WOMEN OF VALOR: Polish Jewish Resisters to
the Third Reich* (WOV/PJ). Those of us who have read and loved—and used it in our
classrooms—are particularly grateful that the youngest of its featured women, Miriam
Brysk, has now partnered with Joanne to write a Young Adult memoir based on her
early childhood experiences during the Holocaust. *A VICTORY FOR MIRIAM! The
Little Jewish Girl Who Defied the Nazis* provides a unique and much-needed example of
a courageous child whose spirit makes her a hero instead of a victim. While this book
was not designed specifically for classroom use, its versatility appeals to a broad range
of educators. As a teacher, a mother, and a student of Holocaust History, I love the
readability and honesty of this book. I highly recommend it for teachers, parents and
grandparents, and students, from 6th to 12th grade—and beyond."

— Sara Melvin,
Certified Holocaust Educator, Clark County School District,
Las Vegas, Nevada

"*A Victory for Miriam!* engages readers of all ages as it reveals the true story
of the underground resistance and how it included Jews of all ages . . .'"

A Victory for Miriam! provides a vivid and compelling account of how a young Jewish
girl who, along with her parents, openly defied the Nazis by becoming active members
of a fierce partisan group. This meticulously researched book immerses the reader in
Miriam's life of constant turmoil, defiance, adaptation, and survival. The reader is drawn
into Miriam's world and her transformation from being an innocent child during the
Nazis' invasion of Poland in 1939, to being a disciplined member of the resistance, then
to her experience as a homeless refugee, and finally, her enrollment as a post-war refugee
in a Brooklyn, New York elementary school. *A Victory for Miriam* engages readers of all
ages and reveals the true story of the underground resistance and how it included Jews
of all ages, entire families, including one very brave little girl. Highly recommended!

— Laura Engel Sahr, MA
Retired, New York State Education Department
Office of Elementary and Secondary Education

"A Victory for Miriam! resonates with a rare and honest view of Jews
who fought the Nazis—and survived!"

Miriam's story is unique in that it provides us with a moving and insightful view of
the partisans from a child's perspective. It is a story of bravery and heroism and the role
that chance or luck or providence plays in everyday life. I was particularly struck by this
story because my family came from Lida, and my cousin was one of the partisans who
snuck into the ghetto to bring people and supplies back to the forest, and I can attest
that Miriam's story rings with authenticity. Her "victory" was due to her strength and
flexibility in overcoming so many obstacles. *Victory* provides young people today with
insights into growing up, friendships, and even the plight of refugees without homes
and without welcome. It shows how children were as deeply affected by the war as were
adults. Miriam's sharing of her story is a gift to all of us.

— Berna Heyman, MLS,
Author of *The Colonel Peter Vroman House: A House with a History*
Retired, Associate Dean of University Libraries
College of William & Mary, Williamsburg, VA

"Miriam's Holocaust "victory," and her many subsequent victories,
sweep the reader into a lifelong journey that truly inspires."

A Victory for Miriam! engages the reader by effectively conveying vivid memories
of war from the clear-eyed perspective of a child . . . It provides a model for overcoming tragedy—even when scars remain from the loss of loved ones. . . The reader is
drawn very close to Miriam, and is almost at one with her through her struggles and
passions. As she weeps, so do we. As she rejoices, so do we. And we share Miriam's
peace when she finally becomes free. Although designed as a book for middle school
youth, *A Victory for Miriam! The Little Jewish Girl Who Defied the Nazis,* is a book
for all ages and stages of life.

— Regina Lederman, Ph.D
Professor Emeritus, University of Texas Medical Branch
Galveston, TX

TABLE OF CONTENTS

A NOTE TO OUR READERS

Welcome to *A Victory for Miriam! The Little Jewish Girl Who Defied the Nazis.* In the decades since World War II ended in 1945, that little girl grew up and became Dr. Miriam M. Brysk: a scientist, medical school professor, graphic artist, loving wife, mother, grandmother, great-grandmother, and dear friend. Miriam's 84th birthday was in March 2019, and as one of the youngest Holocaust survivors,[1] she knows that all too soon there will be no one left to tell the powerful, true stories of one of the most tragic times in history.

It is a tribute to Miriam's great intelligence, courage, and determination, that she is able to share the intense, personal—and often painful—details of her early childhood. Beginning with the bombing of Warsaw when she was only four years old, and continuing through her three years on the run—first from the Nazis and then from the Soviets—Miriam's desperate escapes will have readers cheering her on. Her determination to succeed continued as she faced the strange language, food, customs, and—worst of all—the mean girls at her new school in America. You'll join the audience at Miriam's eighth-grade graduation as they applaud this clear-eyed, courageous young woman who refused to let obstacles stop her. As Miriam's friend and writing partner, I'm happy to let you know that she still refuses to let obstacles stop her!

History books give us facts about Adolf Hitler's determination to eliminate the Jews of Europe both before and during World War II. But facts provide just one view of history. It is also necessary to understand it from the human point of view. The best way to do this is to learn about history from the people who actually experienced it. Miriam and I hope her story will bring history to life for readers and help them gain a deeper understanding of both the evil and the heroism that took place during the Holocaust. And seventy-four years after it ended on May 8, 1945, we hope you will join us in honoring and

---

1 *Holocaust*: (From the Greek: *Holos*=all, *kaustos*=burnt) Also known as the *Shoah* (Hebrew: *catastrophe*), the Holocaust was the period of time between 1933 and 1945 when Germany's Third Reich government, under the leadership of Adolf Hitler, murdered over six-million Jews in its campaign to eliminate the Jews of Europe. A "Holocaust survivor" is someone who lived through this terrible experience.

mourning its over 11 million victims. We especially mourn the more than 1.5 million innocent Jewish children who were victims.

We also honor, celebrate, and learn valuable lessons from those who survived. We are fortunate that Miriam has been willing to relive that horrific time so that others might more fully understand the human reality that gives meaning to the historic facts. I am honored to work with her in creating this book.

Miriam Brysk and I invite you to join us on a journey back in time to her early childhood in Poland during World War II. A time when the Germans almost succeeded in eliminating the entire Jewish population of Europe—including one innocent, determined little girl.

Miriam M. Brysk, Ann Arbor, Michigan
Joanne D. Gilbert, Las Vegas, Nevada
2019

HOLOCAUST OVERVIEW & TIMELINE

Between 1933 and 1945, the German government was known as the *Third Reich* (Empire). Its *Führer* (self-proclaimed leader), Adolf Hitler, was also the leader of the country's all-powerful, ruling political party: the National Socialist German Workers' (Nazi) Party. Hitler had two main goals. The first was to expand the boundaries of Germany by conquering and occupying neighboring countries including Czechoslovakia, Austria, Poland, France, Belgium, Holland, and eventually, the Soviet Union.

Hitler's second goal was to eliminate all the Jewish people in Europe. Hitler called his second goal, "The Final Solution to the Jewish Problem." His campaign to achieve this horrific goal resulted in the deaths of approximately six million Jewish men, women, and children. An additional five million non-Jews also perished. After the end of World War II (1939-1945), Hitler's "Final Solution" became known as the Holocaust, or the *Shoah*, in Hebrew.

Here is a brief overview and timeline of some of the factual events leading up to the most horrific event in modern human history:

JUNE 28, 1919

World War I ended on November 11, 1918, when Germany surrendered to the Allies. It wasn't until June 28, 1919, however, that the Treaty of Versailles was signed by the Allies (the British Empire, France, Russia, Italy, and the United States), and the Central Powers (Germany—under protest, Austria-Hungary, Ottoman Empire and Bulgaria). Germany was angered by this treaty because it stated that Germany had started WWI, and should pay the Allies 33 billion dollars for the costs of the war.

SEPTEMBER 16, 1919

Hitler issued his first written description of Jews as a "race-tuberculosis of the peoples," a deadly, contagious disease that must be eliminated by the government.

FEBRUARY 24, 1920

The National Socialist German Workers' Party (NSDP), known as the Nazi Party, was established. One of its goals was to exclude Jews from the non-Jewish community.

JULY 29, 1921

Adolf Hitler became the leader of the Nazi Party, calling himself: *der Führer.*

NOVEMBER 8-9, 1923

The Munich (Beer Hall) *Putsch* was Hitler's attempt to overthrow the federal government of Germany. When Hitler's attempt failed, he was captured, tried and convicted of treason. It was during his time in prison that he dictated his two-volume book, *Mein Kampf* (My Struggle), in which he outlined his plans for a Germany that would become entirely free of Jewish people.

OCTOBER 24-29, 1929

The crash of the United States Stock Market resulted in the Great Depression, which had a profound impact on the economies of European countries. Still suffering from its defeat in World War I, the German economy went into a devastating decline. Nazi promises of relief from the massive unemployment and poverty began to attract more followers.

JULY 1932

The Nazi party won 37.3% of the vote in the Reichstag elections and became Germany's largest political party.

JANUARY 30, 1933

Hitler was appointed Chancellor of Germany by its President Paul von Hindenburg.

FEBRUARY 27, 1933

A massive fire destroyed the German government's headquarters which were housed in Berlin's Reichstag Building. Many people believed the fire was intentionally set by the Nazis, who then blamed it on the Communist Party. The fire also resulted in the German government's restriction of civil rights.

SEPTEMBER 15, 1935

The Nuremberg Race Laws were passed, taking citizenship away from German Jews, and beginning the legal persecution of the Jewish people.

MARCH 11-13, 1938

The Nazis annexed Austria without resistance. This action was called the Anschluss.

SEPTEMBER 30, 1938

Germany, Great Britain, France, and Italy signed the Munich Agreement giving Germany the Sudetenland region of Czechoslovakia in return for Germany's promise of peace.

NOVEMBER 9-10, 1938

During Kristallnacht, the Night of Broken Glass, Jewish homes, shops, businesses, schools, hospitals, cemeteries, and synagogues across Germany were vandalized, burned and destroyed by Nazi mobs. Almost 100 Jews were killed, and approximately 30,000 Jewish men were sent to Nazi concentration camps. This event marked the first act of mass violence against the Jews of Germany.

AUGUST 23, 1939

The Nazi-Soviet Pact (*Molotov-Ribbentrop Treaty of Non-aggression*) was signed. In this treaty, Hitler and Josef Stalin agreed not to fight each other. They also agreed to divide Poland between their two countries.

SEPTEMBER 1, 1939

Hitler invaded Poland using Blitzkrieg (lightning war) tactics. The Poles fought back, but they were quickly defeated, and Poland was occupied by Germany.

SEPTEMBER 3, 1939

Great Britain and France declared war on Germany.

DECEMBER 11, 1941

The day after Japan's December 7 attack on the U. S. Naval base at Pearl Harbor, Hawaii, the U.S. declared war on Japan. Since Germany, Japan, and Italy were allies, they declared war on the U.S.

JANUARY 20, 1942

The Wannsee Conference held at an estate in Germany, approved the German government's plans for the "Final Solution to the Jewish Problem." This resulted in the construction of the death camps in Poland, and the mass murders of 6 million Jews.

APRIL 30, 1945

After the Allies captured Berlin, Hitler committed suicide.

MAY 7-8, 1945

The Germans surrendered to the Allies, ending World War II in Europe.

PROLOGUE

Would you believe it's been 70 years since I walked across the stage to receive my eighth-grade diploma in January of 1949? That's probably before your Great-grandparents were even born! Funny how even though I've never talked about it with anyone, I still remember it as if it were yesterday . . .

Eighth Grade Graduation—finally! As we stood backstage, fidgeting and trying not to look nervous, my classmates and I waited to hear our names. For us, graduation was a great victory: no more being treated like little kids. We were finally on our way to high school! The world would be ours! Well, at least the high school campus part of the world would be ours. The girls posed awkwardly in their fancy white dresses, grown-up hairstyles, and make-up, as they giggled about boys. The boys slicked their rebellious hair down, fiddled with their ties, and sneakily eyed the suddenly grown-up looking girls. Graduating from eighth-grade caused our emotions to churn. While we were overjoyed to finally be the "big kids," we also were nervous about what lay ahead. And while my feelings about eighth grade graduation were in some ways very similar to my classmates, they were also very different.

Wearing my beautiful white dress and a lovely orchid corsage, I stood silent, alone, and self-conscious, as usual, never quite part of the group. These carefree all-American kids were just going through a regular phase in their regular all-American lives. And even though I'd finally figured out how to dress, walk,

1

and even *almost* talk like them—under the surface, way down where it really counted, we had nothing in common. I was pretty sure that they were all superficial, and totally lacking in any understanding of real life.

Especially my real life.

To them, I was a quiet, serious, alien creature—the girl who talked funny, and didn't understand their jokes. I never was sure when they were making fun of me—something that happened quite often. Even if they had been interested in my real life, how could they possibly have understood what it meant to be a young Jewish Holocaust survivor? No, they couldn't possibly have had any idea of who I was.

Or who I'd been.

Or — for that matter — who I was going to become.

Every single day of my three years in American schools had presented me with at least one opportunity to feel embarrassed—and isolated. I didn't know about American fashion, movie stars, music, "Jitterbug" dancing, 4th of July, Halloween, Thanksgiving, President Truman, or even peanut-butter and jelly sandwiches on tasteless white bread. In other words, every aspect of every day post-World War II American life was totally unfamiliar to me. I did know, however, that I didn't fit in . . . and I wasn't sure I wanted to.

In my *real* life, I was a young Jewish Holocaust refugee,[2] who had been born in Warsaw, Poland in 1935. In 1947, when I was nearly twelve, my family and I arrived in Brooklyn, New York, where I was seen as an ignorant foreigner. I was humiliated to be placed in the 5th grade because I'd had only a few months of formal schooling, and spoke no English. Somehow, in spite of all my deficiencies, I managed to skip a couple of grades, and catch up with my age-group. So, my eighth-grade graduation from an American school, represented far more than just a normal achievement in a regular American life. For me, it also was a victory over my own fears, and my inadequacies, as well as the cruelty of others ranging from Nazis to American "mean girls."

I thought about the Nazis and those mean girls on that bitterly cold January afternoon, when—instead of burrowing into a frozen snowbank in order to hide from murderous Germans, and where—instead of being labelled as a weirdo by

---

2 Refugee: a person who has been forced to escape from his or her homeland because of persecution, violence, war, or natural disaster.

snippy girls, who'd eventually become my friends—I was proudly wearing my lovely white dress, along with my new, not-too-high, white heels, and my first orchid corsage.

The moment of my victory arrived. When my name was finally called, my stomach clenched and lurched. I straightened up as far as my almost five-foot tall body would let me, threw back my shoulders, and managed to walk across the stage toward the extended hand—and smiling face—of our school's principal, Mr. Sammet. I could tell by his big grin and the sparkle in his eye, that he was especially proud to see me walking across that stage. He remembered the bedraggled, awkward and confused young girl he'd welcomed to her first day of seventh grade at Public School 100.

And as I reached out to shake his hand, my past reached out to me telling me to never forget . . .

Chapter 1

March 1935-September 1939: *Early Childhood/Warsaw*

Who could have known on the blustery March day when I was born, that Europe and its Jewish people were about to endure the most brutal and tragic era in human history? Certainly not my excited parents, Dr. Chaim and Bronka Miasnik, or my uncles and aunts—and definitely not my proud new grandparents, who were overjoyed about the arrival of their first grandchild. And for the first four years of my life, our family's joy continued. Life in Warsaw was happy, safe, and full of hope for the future. My parents and I lived in a large, comfortable apartment in a beautiful neighborhood, and we enjoyed our friendly neighbors

My family's first serious warning of the coming Nazi invasion occurred a few days after we returned from our summer vacation at a lovely resort in the country. On August 23, 1939, Germany and the Soviet Union signed the Molotov-Ribbentrop

With my mother, Bronka
Warsaw, Poland: 1935

5

With my mother and father, Chaim
Warsaw, Poland: 1937

Non-Aggression Pact,[3] and jointly took over Poland. Then they went ahead and divided up the country between them. Suddenly, the country of Poland no longer existed. Germany occupied what had previously been the western and central regions of Poland, and the Soviet Union occupied what had once been the eastern region.

Like most little children in Poland—or anywhere else—at that time, I didn't have any idea that a war was coming. Or even what "war" really meant. My family had managed to make my life seem as normal as possible despite the increasingly widespread *antisemitism* in Poland.[4] But on September 1, 1939, when the Germans unleashed their terrifying, deadly airplane attack known as the *Blitzkrieg*, my life, along with the lives of all Poles, especially Jews, abruptly changed. In fact, life as we all had known it, vanished forever—and I quickly learned what war meant.

I remember all too clearly my first bombing experience. It was an ordinary afternoon. I was busy playing with my wooden blocks in our sunny living room. My stomach growled a bit as I inhaled the aroma of the chicken roasting in the kitchen. My young, newly married, Aunt Ala, who was like a second mother to me, sat in a nearby chair, embroidering pillowcases. Then, the last thing that any of us expected—or even could have imagined—happened. Without any warning, our peaceful afternoon was shattered by the deafening roars of German bombers.

Before we could even figure out what we were hearing, we were shaken by the powerful vibrations of bombs as they crashed into our neighborhood. I scrambled up on the sofa and tried to peek out the window, but Aunt Ala, quickly reached over and closed the shutters so I couldn't see outside. She ordered me to scoot under the dining room table, where I sat, paralyzed in fear, until my mother reached down and grabbed me. The hard, determined look on her face frightened me more than the bombs.

---

3 The August 23, 1939, Molotov-Ribbentrop Agreement was signed by former (and future) enemies, Nazi Germany and the Soviet Union. It was a promise that these countries would not attack each other for 10 years. The Germans would break this promise by attacking the Soviets on June 22, 1941.

4 Antisemitism is the hatred of Jewish people.

Without a single word, she and Aunt Ala each grasped one of my hands. When I finally caught my breath, questions flew out of my mouth, "Mama, what's happening? What is all the noise? Why is our house shaking? Where's Papa?"

Mama held my face in her hands, and using my Polish name, responded in a tone of voice I'd never heard. "Mirka, this is serious. It's not a game, and I don't have time to explain. Papa's not here. We must leave this apartment right NOW! No matter what, you must hold on to me or Aunt Ala at all *times*. You must instantly do whatever I tell you, without asking any questions. You must act like a grown-up. Do you understand me?"

Unable to speak, I just nodded solemnly.

We bolted down the five flights of stairs, pushed open the big front door, and ran out onto the street. In a matter of minutes, our safe and friendly block had been transformed into fiery chaos. We became part of a confused, panicked, mob of men, women, and children—all running for our lives. We dodged the bricks, broken glass, and flaming chunks of exploding buildings that hurtled crazily through the air, and plummeted down around us. It was almost like one of today's computer games—except that the targets were us: living, breathing, flesh and blood, panic-stricken human beings.

My Aunt Ala put her arm around me, and held me tightly to her, as we scuffled down the rough, narrow stairs into the crowded basement. The bombing had cut off the electricity, and the subterranean room was so dark that we could barely see each other's faces. We tried—without much success—to avoid stepping on people, as we cautiously made our way through the packed room. With sighs of relief, we found a small space in a corner, where we were able to sit, huddled together. Everyone was nervous, hot, and sweaty, and the foul smells in that dank, dirty, fear-filled cellar made it difficult to breathe. In stark contrast to the deafening pandemonium outside in the streets, the only sounds inside consisted of subdued crying, and the quiet hum of people praying. We all hoped that we would not suffer a direct hit that would have caused the bomb shelter to explode. We also hoped that the tall building above would not collapse and crush us forever.

Wedged tightly together with our families, neighbors, and anyone else who had been nearby when the bombing had started, everyone tried to remain as calm as possible. Even we little kids somehow understood that if one person lost control and started screaming, then everyone else might, also. If anyone was snappish or mean to another person, it might start a fight that would endanger all of us. We understood that the survival of this terrified group depended on each individual being calm, quiet, and considerate of the others. This was a lesson that would serve me well in the coming years.

Luckily, a couple of people had thought to bring flashlights. Once there was a little light, the group began to settle down a bit. My thoughts turned to my father, my uncles, and my grandparents. Worried, I asked Aunt Ala where they all were. She assured me that they all were quite safe in other shelters, and then cradling me in her arms, told me she loved me. I buried my face in her sweet-smelling sweater, and comforted by her calm, loving voice, my eyelids began to droop.

Suddenly, our worst fears became a reality. We were stunned by the deadly whistle of a bomb very close overhead. This was quickly followed by the ear-splitting crash of the building being hit. Everyone held their breaths—waiting for the explosion—and the horror that would follow. But somehow—unbelievably—the bomb did *not* explode! This left us even more dazed and bewildered than before.

What had happened? What would happen next? What should we do? We were completely helpless. Eventually, when we could no longer hear the planes and the bombs, two brave young men—undoubtedly with their hearts beating wildly—set out to see what had happened to the building. They were surprised when they discovered that the five-story staircase was still intact, and they climbed it up to the top floor. Imagine their shock when they slowly opened a door into a bathroom—a bathroom that no longer had a ceiling or a roof—and saw a fat, unexploded bomb sitting calmly in a water-filled bathtub!

A Surprise During the Blitz on Warsaw (Illustration by: Angel L. Luna)

I later learned that some wise person had filled the tub as soon as the bombing had started, in case we would need drinking water. Who knows? Maybe the water had prevented the bomb from detonating. I never found out what they did with it, but to this day, 80 years later, I can never see a bathtub without thinking about that bomb.

After what seemed like forever, but was probably only an hour or so, a man from outside opened the door to the basement and shouted down the stairs that it was all-clear. The bombing had stopped, the planes had gone, and we should go home. As the people filed out, they wondered if they would have homes to go back to. Aunt Ala, Mama, and I held hands, careful not to step on glass or anything that was still burning. Upon reaching our building, we were relieved to see that it was still standing. When we opened the front door, we were further relieved that the inside seemed undamaged, and that the stairs were intact.

Our hopes that our apartment would also be unharmed rose with every stair. And this time, we were lucky. The apartment had suffered only minor damage—probably due to the shaking. Once we had cleaned it up, we realized we were hungry. Then we remembered that there was a chicken in the oven. So there we were, in our normal apartment, at our normal table, eating normal food, and looking at each other in wonder.

What on earth was happening to our world? This was the first time in my life that I realized my mother didn't have all the answers. And this knowledge terrified me as much as the bombing. I expected that my father would have the answers I needed, and I became quite anxious about his whereabouts. When I asked where he and my uncles were, Aunt Ala's response was shocking and scary. She said that they had already left for the city of Lida, where my father was well-known. He had been born and raised there, and as a young man had gone to medical school in nearby Vilnius. Papa and my uncles would be welcomed in Lida because the Soviets desperately needed able-bodied men, especially doctors. In fact, they encouraged Jewish men to leave Nazi-occupied Poland and come to the Soviet sector.

The plan was for Papa and my uncles to find jobs and a place for us all to live. Then, we would leave Warsaw and join them. Amidst the blur of Aunt Ala's words, all I could hear was that *Papa was gone*. What did she mean, Papa was gone? A sick sense of loss filled my stomach as I tried to understand that Papa was far away, but that we would go to him as soon as possible. Unfortunately, it didn't happen soon enough for me.

For the next two weeks, German bombs crashed down on us without mercy, turning our lives upside-down and inside-out. Some days it was impossible to even remember what it was like *not* to be shaken by explosions. *Not* to smell fires and smoke. *Not* to hear the shrill whistle of an incoming bomb right before it hit. When we didn't have time to get to a bomb-shelter, Mama, Aunt Ala, and I would try to squeeze together under our sturdy dining table. Sometimes, Mama would try to calm us down by softly singing her favorite Polish love song, "I Know a Little Street in Barcelona."

I know a little street in Barcelona,
smelling of apple-tree blossom
and I like so much to have a walk there,
whenever I feel tired of a city clamour.
Oh God, how long ago it was
when I was coming here every day to meet
somewhere around the corner
with the first master of my dreams
And I had loved the way I never loved later,
with all my soul and all strength of my heart,
with a springtime joy and youthful inspiration
but unhappily, everything has its end.
Today I return to meet my memories,
to this apple-tree that whispers and say
that I had experienced in its shade
the moments of such a beauty,
that I should not regret my present tears.
—Composer Unknown

When Poland surrendered on September 27, 1939, the Germans flooded into Warsaw. Whether they were driving their trucks up and down our once peaceful, tree-lined streets, or marching in their crisp uniforms and tall, shiny, black leather boots, they seemed to be everywhere. And because of them, life for Jews in Warsaw became increasingly more desperate—and deadly. Even though my mother and Aunt Ala did their best to protect me, my four-year old heart and mind absorbed the tension. I was nervous, confused, and afraid. My father was gone, our city had been bombed, food and water were scarce, and the electricity only worked occasionally. I couldn't go outside to the park, or have friends come to play. And to our shame, we had to wear armbands showing a yellow Star Of David, so everyone would know we were Jews. My mother and Aunt went out only when absolutely necessary to try to find food, and their faces showed the terror they felt. Every time one of them went out, I was afraid she wouldn't return. They probably had the same worry.

Mama and Aunt Ala began to prepare for our trip to Lida. This required secrecy because Jews were no longer allowed to leave Warsaw. Packing was a challenge because we could only take one suitcase each, and we had no idea how long we'd have to stay there. Mama included my blocks and a couple of books in my little suitcase. Throughout this process, I took my cue from Mama and Aunt Ala, and tried to act brave and hopeful. Even at the age of four, I was learning how to keep my emotions hidden.

When the day of our departure from Warsaw arrived, I was excited about reuniting with Papa and my uncles in Lida. I looked forward to us all being safe from the evil Germans and their bombs. Unfortunately, my excitement soon turned into grief. When our tearful relatives gathered in our apartment to say goodbye, it became clear that my grandparents were not coming with us. I felt a sudden pain in my chest, as if my heart were going to burst, and I began to wail uncontrollably.

Mama told me that I had to stop crying because we were leaving at that moment. A group of crying Jews would make it obvious that we were leaving, and we could be arrested. My grandparents tried to console me by saying that they would write often, and they asked me to draw and send them pictures of our life in Lida. I managed to calm down a bit and hung on tight to each one as I was passed back and forth between my weeping relatives.

As we walked to the station, I almost tripped when I looked back over my shoulder, waving sadly to my grandparents' fading faces in the window. When we arrived at the train's crowded platform, I was surprised by how quiet it was. Instead of the usual hustle bustle, no one seemed to be talking to anyone else. There was no laughing or sense of excitement. Mama, Aunt Ala, and I were also quiet—each of us lost in our own troubled thoughts.

All too soon it was time to board the train. Since it was important not to appear or sound Jewish, Mama cautioned me to only whisper to her and Aunt Ala, and not to talk to anyone else. She was afraid that I might accidentally say something that would cause us to be arrested for trying to leave Warsaw. Just as we climbed the steps to board the train, Mama brought me close to her, and much to my shock, she removed my armband with the yellow Jewish Star. She put her index finger to her lips, reminding me to remain silent. I notice that she and Aunt Ala no longer wore their armbands.

Once on board, we found our seats, and began our 10+ hour journey. We were headed east, to what had recently become the German-Soviet border. I pressed my teary face against the cold window, while Mama patted my back, urged me to "hush," and assured me that we'd return home soon.

Contrary to Mama's bravely optimistic assurances, however, we did not return to Warsaw soon. And we never saw my grandparents again.

Strolling Along the Wistula

I made this collage in 2006 showing my beloved grandparents, Ita and Avrum Zablocki, in 1939 before the war. The barely visible, peaceful scene of Warsaw's beautiful Wistula River symbolizes the fading memory of normal life. My grandparents were soon confined to the Warsaw ghetto on Pawia Street, and then deported to Treblinka where they were murdered.

I made this artwork from a photo taken in August 1939, just before the war broke out. The faded lines and lack of boundaries foreshadow the coming chaos.

Shattered Childhood
(2006)

Chapter 2

October 1939: *Life in Soviet Lida*

Lida was a small, bustling city in the eastern region of Poland, and it had a large, thriving, Jewish population. In fact, of its 19,000 people, one-third (6,300) were Jewish, and despite their different religions, everyone usually got along pretty well. That changed when the Germans occupied western Poland, and so many terrified Jews fled to the east. Since Lida was in the east, and now under Soviet control, its Jewish population began to grow quickly. Every day brought more and more Jewish refugees. Including us.

I don't remember anything from our train trip to Lida—I think I was so exhausted from crying, that the sound and motion of the train quickly lulled me to sleep. But I'll never forget that when we finally arrived at the station, Papa managed to swoop me up in his arms and hug Mama at the same time. I wrapped my little arms around his neck as tightly as I could, breathed in his familiar smell, and felt safe for the first time in two months. Papa took us straight to the house which he and my Uncle Tadek had inhabited since they'd arrived in Lida, and where we would all would now live.

Over our first dinner together since the German invasion, the men told us scary stories about the dangers they'd faced when they'd fled Warsaw for Lida. Even though I could see them safe and secure right in front of me, I still trembled in fear when they recounted their near-death escapades, hiding in shadows, sleeping in barns, and getting lost at night. They'd run out of food by the third day, so they'd had to steal whatever they could from farmers' fields.

Even though they hid during the day, they were sometimes spotted, and shot at, so they had to be ready to run for their lives at a moment's notice. They had to leap into rivers in order to escape vicious dogs, and so their clothes were usually wet and caked with mud. Despite my terror at their stories, I somehow managed to fall asleep at the table. Papa carried me to the bed that the three of us would now share. This arrangement was just fine with me. I liked having my parents nearby, where I could see that they were safe. I'm not so sure they appreciated my company—it wasn't a large bed!

Even though I had no clue about what was going on, I shared my family's relief and happiness that we had escaped the Germans. We were grateful to be living in Lida, under the rule of the Soviets, although they weren't particularly kind to us. At least they weren't trying to murder us just because we were Jewish. Plus, they allowed Jews to work, so our living conditions were not as desperate as they had been in Warsaw. Unfortunately, along with this happiness came a great sadness. One of the able-bodied men the Soviets wanted in their army was mother's brother, Sevek. A few days after escaping Warsaw with Papa and Uncle Tadek, he was drafted into the Soviet army and sent far away to fight Germans. We never saw him again.

Papa was warmly welcomed to work at the hospital since the staff, remembered him with affection from his days there as a medical student. He began performing surgeries, and became highly respected for his skill and compassion. My uncle Tadek also found a job as welder. Our days felt safe, and we waited hopefully for the Germans to leave Poland so we could go home to Warsaw.

Of course, there were the occasional bad surprises—like on the first day I went out to play. Mama had carefully dressed me in one of my pretty, stylish, short-skirted outfits from Warsaw. She had assured me that I looked beautiful, and that I'd make new friends soon. Feeling confident, I cheerfully skipped out the door, eager to meet and play with the neighborhood children. I was in for a rude awakening.

Imagine my mother's surprise when within two minutes, I rushed back into the house sobbing. The neighborhood girls had taken one look at me, and burst into shrieks of laughter, making my spirits sink. The girls screamed what sounded like insults at me in Yiddish—a language I didn't yet understand. But I could tell from their tone, their sing-songy voices, and their pointing fingers, that something about me was completely ridiculous. When one of them finally switched to Polish—which I did understand—my spirits sank even further.

"Hey little girl, why are you wearing such a short little baby dress?"

"Hey, you! You—with the skinny legs and knobby knees!"

"Why don't you answer us?"

"Haven't you learned to talk yet?"

I tearfully tried to explain the problem to Mama and Aunt Ala. Fortunately, they made the situation seem so silly, that we all ended up laughing. I was relieved that instead of going outside and yelling at the girls—which would have made me look like even more of a baby—Mama took out her sewing box, and began to lengthen my dresses. Once I didn't look like a foreigner—or a baby— the girls became kinder to me, and eventually, became my friends. They even let me hang around with them, and taught me how to speak Yiddish.

With our safety assured, and our basic needs met, our family settled into a routine. During the days, Mama and Aunt Ala cooked and baked and did their best to make the house warm and homey. They wanted to make sure that when the men came home from work, they'd be comfortable and have a good meal.

Despite all the terrible things that were going on in Poland, the grown-ups did their best to make our lives seem normal. So at least to me, life was peaceful under the Soviet Occupation. But what did I know? Life can be simple when you're five years old. To me, "peaceful" meant that no Germans were bombing us. As long as no one was blowing us up, life seemed normal. Throw in the occasional piece of candy, and I was happy.

Something else that made me happy was learning to read and write from Mama and Aunt Ala. I also enjoyed feeling like a grown-up when I helped them with whatever cooking and household chores I could manage. We had warm clothes, enough food, and thanks to Papa, we also had medical care when needed. Our house had indoor plumbing, electricity, and a stove, as well as a metal box which could keep food cool for a day or two. Because of Papa's surgical skills, and kindness to his patients, our family also enjoyed a high degree of respect from other Jews, as well as Gentiles, and even the Soviets. We were grateful to have a better living standard than most of the other western Polish Jews who had fled to Lida.

Our daily life was totally different from what it had been in Warsaw. First, and foremost, of course, there were no Germans bombing us—yet. And while we lived in the Jewish section of Lida, we were still able to move freely through the whole town. There was no curfew for us, and we didn't have to wear Stars of David to let everyone know we were Jews. So from my point of view, we had every reason to think that life was normal.

Each morning, the men got up before we did, made their own breakfasts, packed their own lunches, and left for work. Mama, Aunt Ala, and I would snuggle in bed under Mama's soft goose down-comforter a little longer. Then we'd have breakfast, and start the day's housework: dusting sweeping, and hand-washing our laundry in a big wash tub. When our indoor chores were completed, we'd work in the garden. On the weekends, we'd go shopping at the large outdoor market in the center of town. Everyone on the streets exchanged friendly greetings, and sometimes a shopkeeper would give me a little treat. When the weather was nice, Mama and I would walk to the nearby orchard where we picked crisp, delicious, apples, and gathered sweet, juicy berries. We triumphantly presented our harvest to Aunt Ala so she could make her much-appreciated, mouth-watering pastries. After lunch, I'd go out and play with my friends until Mama called me in for dinner.

Each day's biggest joy was when the men came home, washed up, and joined us for the wonderful meal that my mother and Aunt Ala had prepared. We had lively conversations about our day's activities and adventures. Since the grown-ups always made a point of listening attentively to my reports, and asking me for more details, they made me feel valued and important. After cleaning up, it was time for me to get ready for bed. I looked forward to nestling under Mama's cozy comforter as I listened to the bed-time stories she or Aunt Ala would read to me. After hugs and kisses, I'd drift off to a peaceful sleep—a sleep that was no longer interrupted by Nazi nightmares.

My only sadness was that my grandparents weren't with us. For a while, we sent letters to them, but this became more and more difficult because the Nazis' mail-censors read every word, looking for secret codes and anti-Nazi messages. If they didn't like what they read, they could have the recipients arrested. So, instead of highly detailed, multi-page letters, we sent postcards with short messages. We continued sending these postcards long after responses stopped coming.

On June 22, 1941, when I was just six-years old, our happy days came to a shocking and brutal end. We didn't know it then, but this was the day that the Germans had suddenly broken their non-Aggression Treaty (the *Molotov-Ribbentrop Agreement*) with the Soviet Union, by viciously attacking from the sky. Since Lida was located in what was at that time the Soviet Union, we once again were targets for the Nazis. So once again we heard the roars of low-flying planes as they circled above us before dropping hundreds of whistling bombs. My recently forgotten memories of the terror in Warsaw came flooding back.

It was early on a warm, sunshiny morning, and the men had just left for work. We "women" still hadn't gotten out of bed, and were lazily enjoying that sweet interlude between sleep and wakefulness. Without warning, we were jolted out of our warm snuggle by the deafening roar of what I instantly knew were bomber planes flying directly overhead.

"Mama, what's going on? Are we being attacked again?"

Mama did not immediately respond. Shaken, we huddled closely together, somehow drawing strength from each other's presence. I choked back tears as Mama took both of my hands and looked me right in the eyes, trying with the strength of her gaze to calm me down. She explained that the Germans were attacking Lida, and we were once again in the middle of a war zone.

"Don't worry, Mirele, we will be all right. Remember in Warsaw, when you had to follow my orders immediately and without question? We came out all right then, and we will be all right this time, too."

And just like in Warsaw, her voice became strange as she continued, "No matter what happens, no matter how frightened you might be, do exactly what I tell you. Do not ask questions. Talk only to Aunt Ala or to me." Remembering the last time I'd heard these directions, I felt a familiar burning rush of panic, and then I turned ice cold in spite of our comforter. Holding back all of the questions that threatened to burst out of my head, I nodded my agreement.

I now had another day I would never forget.

This time, unlike the bombing of Warsaw, where we had lived in a sturdy, brick and cement apartment building, we now lived in a small, wooden house. And it shook violently. Through our windows, Mama, Aunt Ala, and I could see the houses around us bursting into flames. Mama told us that we needed to move fast, so we grabbed our sweaters, and hurried out of the house.

Holding hands, we ran toward the outskirts of town, and then on to the farmland that lay a couple of miles further. In the midst of the explosions, and the flames, as well as the terrorized people, pets, and livestock, my biggest fear was that I might get separated from Mama and Aunt Ala. I was even more terrified than I'd been in Warsaw, because now I was older, and understood the dangers. Also, I wasn't as easily comforted by the words of my elders. Nothing they could say would calm my fear of possibly having to manage on my own in this chaos.

We were engulfed by other frenzied townspeople who were also escaping as fast as they could. It was like a churning, human flood—all of us surging away from the center of town. It seemed as if we ran for hours, dodging bombs, fires, exploding buildings, broken glass—and death. During that whole time, even after we no longer could feel the heat of our burning city on our backs, we didn't look back once. We just kept our eyes focused on any possible escape routes ahead of us.

Unlike many of the other exhausted escapees who had already stopped in the farmland, my mother wasn't taking any chances on our safety. We'd continued further into the wild, uninhabited fields beyond the farms. Finally, unable to go another step, we sank to the ground. Only after I'd settled into my mother's lap, did I ask her if we really could get away from the Germans this time. Instead of answering my question directly, she held me tight, and assured me that we would be all right. What could any mother have said in those circumstances?

Suddenly, the bombing just stopped. It seemed as if all sound had been sucked out of the world. The abrupt, eerie, utter silence was almost as frightening as the ear-spitting bombing. It was as if we'd gone deaf. Adding to this unearthly atmosphere were the fiery streaks of the setting sun, which created an ironic rainbow of horror as they sliced through the smoky sky. Little by little, the people around us began to stir and stand up. I could hear men, women, and children crying out for help, and calling out the names of missing loved ones.

Mama, Aunt Ala, and I stood up, brushed our clothes off, hugged each other tightly, and holding hands, began our long walk back to town. We stepped cautiously through the smoldering ruins of Lida, trying not to look at—or hear—the dead and dying. Our irritated eyes burned and watered from the ash-filled air. Afraid to speak the words out loud, we could feel each other's dread about what we would find when we got home. Would there even be a home to return to? Would Papa and my uncle be safe?

Imagine the waves of mixed feelings that hit us when we turned the corner and saw that amidst the smoking, crumbled ruins of our neighborhood, only one house was still standing—and it was ours! Propelled by joy and relief, we rushed forward, eager to feel the comfort and safety of home. These feelings were overshadowed, however, by grief at the sight of our dazed and weeping neighbors as they carefully sifted through the ruins of what had once been their homes.

And then, just as suddenly, another wave of emotion flooded us with joy when we opened our front door and saw Papa and my uncle sitting at the dining table. They were waiting for us just as if we were returning late from a shopping trip! There was food on the table, and the room was lit by candles. It was beautiful—just like a photograph in a magazine!

Can you imagine it? My beloved Papa and uncle, sitting at the table in a lovely, candle-lit dining room—right in the midst of the sights, sounds, and smells of a smoldering war zone! I practically flew into Papa's arms and wouldn't let go. Everyone hugged and cried. Then, after washing up, we sat at the table and breathlessly told the men what had happened to us, and what we'd seen. With me safely nestled in his lap—a lap which I fully intended to never leave, Papa told us what it had been like at the hospital during the bombardment. Instead of going to a bomb shelter, he had stayed to provide emergency care to his patients, as well as injured townspeople, and—reluctantly—even some injured Germans. My uncle had left his job to come to get us, but seeing that our house was empty, he'd rushed out of town, hoping to find us in the countryside.

There was some damage to our house, but we would be able to clean it up. Life would go on. Before long, feeling warm and safe, I fell asleep in my father's arms, at which point, he gently carried me to bed, carefully uncurled my fingers from his shirt, and tucked me in. I burrowed down, warm and safe. All too soon, I wouldn't even be able to remember what feeling warm and safe was.

On Friday, June 27, 1941, just five days after the bombing, German ground-troops entered the city. By the next day, which was Saturday (the Jewish Sabbath, or day of rest), the Germans had completely occupied Lida. There were brutal looking, brutal sounding, and brutal acting Germans everywhere. They hadn't yet begun enforcing specific anti-Jewish laws, but just to let us know that we were under their control, they murdered 80 Jews. Thereafter, just the sight of their crisp, clean uniforms, tall, shiny, black leather boots, deadly guns, and their unblinking, robot eyes, struck terror into our hearts. We tried to adjust to this new reality, and went about our lives as normally as possible, but this new "normal" had become constant terror.

One day, something even more unusual and terrifying than the everyday unusual and terrifying did happen. Mama and I were walking home from our usual trip to the outdoor market, when a German officer suddenly approached us on the street. Our feet froze to the sidewalk, and our hearts stood still. We tried to breathe normally, especially when he smiled and lifted me into his arms, and tenderly brushed my hair out of my face. Speaking German, he told my mother about his own beautiful little girl back home, and how much he missed her. It seemed like such a normal situation, but it only happened because my mother and I didn't look Jewish. If the officer had known we were Jews, he probably would have killed us on the spot. We didn't start breathing normally until we got home. Needless to say, after that, Mama left me at home when she went shopping.

On that day, good timing and good luck saved our lives. The very next week, however, good timing and good luck were in short supply. The Germans ordered all Jews to sew yellow Stars of David on the fronts and backs of our clothing. That way we could be easily identified and treated according to the brutal whims of any German who spotted us. Even as a young child, I was observant, thoughtful, and curious. Facts were important to me. I wanted to know exactly what was so bad about Jews that we had to be identified so easily. Why did so many Poles and Soviets hate us? Why did the Germans actually want to kill us? Were we different from other people? We seemed like such nice, normal, loving people to me.

The increasingly harsh, constantly changing anti-Jewish laws increased our stress and panic to an unbearable level. Jews had been a vibrant and important part of Lida's history since the 10th century, but now that we were officially, and visibly, labelled as being less than human—no Jew was safe anywhere in Lida.

As terrible as conditions were, our family continued to be a little better off than others because Papa's position at the hospital gave him access to food and medical supplies. We were also grateful that since Papa was the best surgeon in the city, he was respected by the Germans—on whom he was often called upon to operate. And while he hated having to provide medical care for the Germans, he knew that we were relatively safe as long as his patients recovered.

By the second week in July, the Nazis established a *Judenrat*—or Jewish Council. This was a group of 10-15 Jewish men who were put in the impossible position of having to enforce all Nazi orders against the Jews. These included enforcing orders against their own families, friends, and neighbors— by any means necessary. Some members of the Judenrat risked their lives to help other Jews whenever possible. They tried to alert a person who was about to be arrested, and they sent out warnings of upcoming deadly Nazi attacks, known as *aktions*, on the Jewish community. Another group of Jewish men was ordered to become the Nazis' police force in Lida. Some members of Judenrat and Jewish police force chose to commit suicide rather than obey the Nazis' orders. Others were not so noble.

The next wave of directives made life almost impossible. Jews were not allowed to practice their religion. Jews were not allowed outside after curfew. Jews had to get off the sidewalk and walk in the dusty or muddy street if a German was walking near them. Jews were not allowed to gather in groups, and Jewish children were no longer allowed to attend public schools. As always, Mama tried to make our lives feel normal. She reassured me that all would be well eventually—but until eventually came, we never knew when something terrible would happen. In fact, it was more of a surprise when something terrible didn't happen.

My constant questions about why we were hated so much must have been an endless challenge for my parents. I'm sure they were also hoping to find answers to the same questions. Whatever it was that was bad about us, it must have been really bad, because one day in early July 1941, all of Lida's Jewish professionals, the city's most prominent and respected lawyers, teachers, and doctors—even my Papa—were ordered to report to Nazi headquarters. We had no idea what was going to happen to them. Then, on July 5, all but a few of them were shot to death. For no reason. Those who were allowed to live had been identified as being "useful" to the Nazis. Until Papa walked back through our door, we didn't know that he had been allowed to live. Because he was a surgeon, he was considered to be useful. This would not be the last time my father's position as a surgeon would save our lives.

For this picture, I surrounded a 1939 photo of my mother that had been taken in the Lida ghetto, by images of the postcards and stamps. This was to show that Jews were trapped, totally isolated and unable to communicate with the outside world.

Stamps of Oppression
(2006)

Chapter 3
December 1941: *The Lida Ghetto*

In the fall of 1941, the Germans started removing poverty-stricken Christian residents from their homes in Lida's three poorest neighborhoods. This action was taken because the Germans were preparing the area to become a prison-like Jewish ghetto.[5] This separate, fenced-in and gated section of town was patrolled night and day by brutal armed guards and their vicious dogs. At the beginning of December, when the Germans were confident that the ghetto was escape-proof, they drove trucks with loudspeakers up and down Lida's streets, blaring the announcement that all the Jews of Lida should immediately leave their homes. Thunderstruck, Jewish families didn't even have time to think. They rushed to put on as many layers of clothing as they could. They stuffed their pockets with valuables, shoes, reading-glasses, hair-brushes, food, medicines, important papers, and precious photographs. We could take only what we could grab. Everything else had to be left behind, and was later either stolen by looters or confiscated by the Germans.

As we exited through the front door, we were ordered to join the massive line of Jews already in the street. At first we all moved like a river of slowly flowing lava—then, in response to the Germans' painful kicks, blows and gun-shots, we all walked as fast as we could across town. With the enthusiasm of crazed

---

5 The word *"ghetto"* is generally thought to have originated in Venice, Italy in the early 1500s. The city leaders decided that Jews should be required to live in a small area on one of Venice's islands. They called it the "Ghetto Nuova." The word, "ghetto," has several possible meanings, but in this case, it refers to the area or street where Jews are forced to live. "Nuova" means, "new."

cattle-drivers, the Germans herded all 4,000 of Lida's Jews toward the small, newly created ghetto. During this process, the soldiers had fun punching, kicking, and pushing handicapped, elderly, and slow-moving Jews—laughing at them as they tried desperately to keep up with the rest of us. My parents, uncle, and Aunt Ala carefully surrounded me as we walked, making sure to hold my hands so I wouldn't be torn away and trampled. They also tried to keep me from seeing what was going on, but I could hear the sobbing and screaming and the gunshots when some unfortunate person had been unable to move fast enough.

Grouped as families, and under the watchful eyes of the Germans, our terrified and confused procession plodded on, having no idea what awaited us. As we entered the ghetto, we were stunned to see it was totally empty. It was as if all its former residents had just evaporated. Whenever we came to a house, the Germans would randomly shove several families into it, and then everyone else would move on to the next house. With sinking hearts, we realized that we would now be living in what had once been someone else's home. I wondered what had happened to those people. Did they have a little girl? Was she as frightened as I was? I also wondered if strangers would now be moving into the house we'd just left on the other side of the ghetto fence.

When we first saw the ramshackle little five-room house that was assigned to us, we were relieved that at least it seemed big enough for five people. Our relief didn't last long, however, because we were soon joined by three other families, that had also been assigned to this one little house. Each room would be shared by as many people as could be packed in. There was a living-dining room, a non-working kitchen, and three small bedrooms, but unfortunately no indoor bathroom. Mama, Papa, and I shared one little bedroom with Aunt Ala and Uncle Tadek—four adults and a child in one tiny room. And we were luckier than most because our family was so small.

Similar crowding was taking place throughout the ghetto because all of Lida's 4,000 Jews were being forced to live in fewer than 100 houses. With up to five or even more families of varying sizes now being crammed into each rat-infested dwelling, you can imagine the emotions that threatened to erupt. Somehow, however, everyone did their best to be as cooperative as possible in deciding which families would live in which room. Some families even had to live in kitchens, which of course weren't being used for cooking because they no longer had running water or electricity. If there had been an indoor bathroom, some family would probably have had to live in it.

Speaking of bathrooms, as soon as we had moved into our room, I whispered to Mama that I really had to "go." She took my hand, and led me out to the

backyard in the hopes of finding an outhouse. With a mixture of relief and horror, we found it. Inside the rickety, claustrophobic, wooden outhouse, the overpowering stench choked me and made my eyes water. The so-called toilet was
actually a filthy, splintery, wooden box, approximately three feet high. It was
definitely not built with a child in mind, and it was really hard for me to hoist
myself up on it. Then, once I got there, things got really scary, because it was
strategically placed over a deep, hideously stinking, totally open pit. The toilet
"seat" consisted of a rough board with a hole in it.

We were supposed to balance ourselves above the hole and relieve ourselves—failure to do this just right could result in a bottom with splinters. This
was not an easy task for a frightened little girl who was in a hurry, and holding
her breath. My worst fear was that I would fall in to that pit of putrid horror,
and no one would ever know what had happened to me. I'd just be swallowed
up in the reeking muck. Thereafter, I tried to go to the outhouse as infrequently
as possible. When I couldn't avoid going, I'd take a deep breath before entering,
and hold it until I'd escaped back out into the fresh air.

Inside our ghetto house, there was little furniture because the previous owners had taken whatever they could, and then thieves had stolen the rest. We were
lucky that our tiny room still had a bed, which we took turns sharing. Sometimes
Mama, Papa, and I would squeeze into the bed together. Anyone who didn't get
a place on the bed just slept on the floor. We were always climbing over each
other. There was absolutely no privacy. The walls of the house were thin, and the
constant sights, smells, and sounds of frightened, over-worked, dirty, sick and
dying humans was overwhelming.

And everyone was hungry—all the time. The Germans rationed our daily
food allotment to fewer than 600 calories. This was half of what a normal
person needed to survive. We weren't allowed to drink milk, or eat meat,
butter or eggs. If a Jew looked too healthy, he or she could be suspected
of stealing food, and subject to arrest. We were a little luckier than most
because our house's previous occupants had planted a vegetable garden in
the backyard behind the barn. So we were able to find some potatoes and
onions, with which Mama could cook a watery soup over a small fire in the
back yard. Without that little garden, we would have starved to death—as
so many others did.

Soon, Jewish men ages 15 and older were registered, and then sent on
exhausting, degrading work assignments where they were often beaten for
no particular reason, and under the constant threat of death. The long work-
day, usually outdoors in all kinds of weather, was brutal. Duties included
breaking rocks into gravel, building roads and bridges, sweeping snow,

clearing out and rebuilding damaged buildings—sometimes these were their own former homes—outside the ghetto. They were given almost no food—usually just a slice of stale bread and a bowl of so-called "soup," made of rotten potatoes.

Ironically, living in one small house with so many people made us feel both over-crowded and isolated. With so many people squeezed together, there was no privacy. We were physically crowded, but emotionally, very separated. Since everyone could hear, see, and smell everything that was going on—we had to pretend that we didn't. In order to prevent arguments and fights, we took care to be very polite. We learned to keep our thoughts, opinions, and problems to ourselves.

Each day brought us closer to starvation, but as before, since Papa was an important surgeon, our family was a little luckier than the others. Papa continued working at the hospital outside of the ghetto, and he now had to wear a white armband with a red cross on it, indicating he was a doctor. Little did we know that this armband would soon save our lives. While Papa's position forced him to give medical care to Germans, it also allowed him to secretly help sick and wounded Jews. Along with this benefit, however, came the terror that if one of Papa's German patients had a complaint, or failed to heal—or heaven forbid, *died*—we'd be immediately killed.

Despite the danger and miserable conditions, for a little while longer, I still possessed the innocence of a young child. I still believed that my all-powerful parents, as well as Aunt Ala, and Uncle Tadek, would protect me from danger. No matter how wretched our living circumstances were, I felt safe as long as I had them nearby. This sense of safety ended with a new directive ordering all women over age 16 to report for work. This meant that Mama and Aunt Ala would no longer be able to take care of me. I'd never been left without adult supervision before, and I was terrified by the prospect of being alone.

Fortunately, there was another little girl in the house. Her name was Tuska. With no adults to take care of us, Tuska and I quickly learned to depend on each other. We were responsible for fixing our own meals—usually just a piece of bread—and keeping our family's rooms neat. We had to stay out of sight so that no Germans would see us. We were both terrified that soldiers would come and hurt us or take us away.

Despite the dire circumstances, my friendship with Tuska brightened my days. It's amazing what having a friend can do! On our own, we were just two frightened six-year-olds, but together we seemed older—and braver. To the best of our ability, we watched out for each other, providing comfort if either of us got hurt or was sad. We spent most of our time playing outside in the backyard, where we wouldn't be seen. One of our favorite games was trading the labels we'd remove from bottles and cans. We would find these cans by rummaging through piles of garbage. I was luckier than she was at this because my father worked outside the ghetto and always brought me nice clean labels!

Even though we had fun playing our little games, we were never actually carefree. We had been well-trained, and knew that if we were forgetful, we would endanger ourselves as well as our families. We had to be careful about more things than we could count. At all times we had to worry about making noise, going into the front yard, being hungry, being sick, being abandoned, being taken prisoner, being tortured . . . being executed. We could never forget that a catastrophe could happen without any reason, at any minute, to any and to all of us.

I also had to be careful to hide my emotions from everyone, even my parents and Aunt Ala. I didn't have the freedom to laugh or cry. A crying little kid would not have been appreciated by adults who were desperately trying to keep that little kid and themselves alive. Of course I still felt confusion, terror, sadness, anger, and hurt, but I learned to bury these feelings. And I became very good at it. In fact, I buried them so far down inside me, that I didn't realize how much power they held over me until decades later, when I was a grown up, and free to cry. But by then, I had no tears left.

Today, whenever I see happy, healthy, young American children innocently playing, I can't help but flash back to when I was that age. I picture today's children in my circumstances—hungry, without adult supervision or protection, and in constant danger of death. Unlike me, these lucky six-year-olds are free to show emotions by laughing and crying—and unbeknownst to them, they also enjoy the glorious freedom from worry about constant danger.

The ghetto became increasingly crowded with Jews from the surrounding region who were fleeing the dangers of their own villages. Along with increased crowding, each day brought more cruelties for us to adjust to—along with rumors of more horrors to come. One day, the hideous rumors became a hideous reality. On May 7, 1942, the ghetto was "sealed." This meant that no one was allowed in or out. It was surrounded by savage local Lida police and merciless German *Gestapo* agents, as well as Hitler's particularly vicious Stormtroopers,[6] and local collaborators. This was a new development. And it was terrifying. What was going to happen to us now?

6 The *Gestapo*, or *Geheime Staatspolizei*, were the secret police of Nazi Germany and German-occupied Europe. The Stormtroopers were Hitler's vicious, semi-military group.

What happened would forever after be known as the "Great Jewish Massacre of Lida." Just as dawn was breaking on May 8, 1942—a morning that was still so cold from winter that there was snow on the ground—life for the almost 6,000 Jewish residents of the Lida ghetto became hell on earth. Nazis stormed into the ghetto like a frenzied mob of butchers, thirsting for Jewish blood. Screaming obscenities at the top of their lungs, they ordered us all to get out of our houses and onto the street. Most of us weren't even dressed yet. My mother put my coat on over my pajamas, and grabbed my shoes and socks. As the Jews left the shelter of their homes, we were ordered to line up in family groups and walk in silence until we were told to stop. Anyone who lagged, stepped out of line, or made any noise, would be beaten or shot on the spot. There was no doubt that this would be the end of our lives.

Every once in a while, the silence was broken by an escaping sob. We had no idea what our destination would be, or how long it would take to get there. Nearly 6,000 Jewish men, women, and children all walked in silent dread—some people with cold, bare, bleeding feet. I knew better than to ask my parents any questions. Around noon, after walking for hours, the group was ordered to stop and line up at the intersection of two country roads. We could hear the spine-chilling clatter of rifle-fire beyond some nearby trees. The German District Commissioner and his assistants stood at the front of the line and began examining everyone's identification papers. After each inspection, the person was directed to go to either the right or the left. Aunt Ala and Uncle Tadek, who were in front of us, were sent to the left—away from the gunshots.

My parents and I were sent to the right—toward the nonstop sharp cracking sounds of rifle shots. The Nazis continued to beat us, while screaming that we must go faster and faster. My parents held each of my arms as we ran toward our deaths. Sometimes my feet left the ground, and I was swung like a doll between them as they ran. Somehow, amidst the chaos, we didn't immediately hear a soldier shouting at us to halt and go back. He kept shrieking, "*Arzt zuruek!*"—"*Doctor, go back, go back!*"—over and over. When we didn't react to him, he ran up, grabbed Papa's arm, pointed at his red-cross armband, and ordered him to turn back.

You can imagine the confusion—and then numb relief—we felt at this abrupt change of plans. At that moment, Mama and I were grateful that at least Papa would be saved. We thought that we would still be shot. To our surprise, the soldier indicated that all three of us should come with him! I've always wondered how that dirty, four-inch-wide, red-and-white arm-band caught the Nazi's attention. A fragile piece of tattered fabric—and the acute vision of a German soldier—saved our lives that day.

We gratefully rejoined Aunt Ala and Uncle Tadek in the small group that had been chosen to live. Sobbing, we grabbed at each other in a frenzy, and held on for dear life. The Germans soon ordered us all to be silent, and then directed us to lie down on the ground so that they could count the survivors. After the count, they commanded us to stand up, and bow to the Germans to show our appreciation at being spared. Then, as the sun set, we were led back into our ghetto.

We were stunned by what awaited us. It was a ghost-town, inhabited only by the phantoms of those who had just been murdered. The Germans had stormed into the empty ghetto and executed anyone they found hiding. They also took any remaining valuables they could find. Fortunately, my parents had already buried their valuables, including some gold coins and their wedding rings, under the step just inside the barn's door, so there was nothing left for the looters to take.

Our relief at being allowed to live another day was mixed with sorrow when we learned that all the others, those who had been sent to the right—numbering more than 4,000—had immediately been shot. Fifteen hundred others had been allowed to live because they were strong and healthy enough to be useful to the Germans. As a surgeon, my father was considered to be especially "useful." We'll never know why my mother and I were also spared.

Although we weren't surprised that the inside of our house had been totally trashed by the Germans searching for valuables, it was a shock to see everything torn apart. My parents, Aunt, Uncle, and I gazed around us in speechless horror. Suddenly, none of this mattered to me because standing in the doorway of her family's room, her wide-eyed face smeared with dirt and tears, was Tuska. Somehow her family had also been chosen to live. As our little bodies clung to each other, the emotions we hadn't been allowed to express erupted, and we wept uncontrollably. For the next few days, the only time we were separated was when we slept.

The eerie emptiness of the Lida ghetto did not last long. It soon became even more crowded than it had been before the massacre. This was because the Germans were removing the Jews from all the other towns in our region, and putting them in one central location: Lida. We didn't know it then, but the future of all the Jews in Lida was grim. In fact, there was no future. By September 18, 1943, they all would be deported or exterminated. This would be the last step in the Nazis' process of eliminating all the Jews of the region. Then they would be able to declare with pride, that they had reached their goal: the region would be, *Judenfrei*—free of Jews.

Conditions worsened by the day—especially in the frigid winter when there was no heat. People huddled together to try to keep from freezing. And whenever they got a chance, they would search for wooden furniture that they could break apart and use for firewood. It seemed as if everyone was sick, starving, and freezing in the bitter winter.

When we woke up each morning, the first thing we did was peek out the window to look for Germans. They would often bang on someone's front door, order all the occupants to go outside, and then execute them. If we didn't see any Germans outside, we hoped it meant that we would not die that day. And that's how we lived. One day at a time. Sometimes one hour at a time. Living so close to death made dying just a part of our daily existence. And while it no longer shocked us, we hoped to avoid it for as long as possible.

Within this world of misery, the Lida ghetto's residents were just a little bit luckier than other ghettos—at least for a while. This was because Lida was an industrialized city, and many of its Jewish workers were highly skilled in their trades. One day, the leader of the Judenrat took a big risk by approaching the Germans to suggest that the Jews could help them by setting up small workshops. These would be used for manufacturing shoes, gloves, electrical supplies, clothing, paintings, toys, handbags, briefcases—anything that the Germans needed for themselves, or could send back to their families in Germany, or to make money by selling. Fortunately, the Germans agreed: and allowed Jews to set up small workshops in a group of vacant buildings, just outside the ghetto's walls.

These little factories were known as *Handverkshtaten*, in German, or "workshops where things were made by hand." The products were particularly attractive to the Germans because whatever their petrified prisoners made would be of the best quality—and would cost nothing! My mother worked in a shop making leather belts and wallets. My uncle worked as a welder. These workshops were so successful that German newspapers sent reporters all the way from Berlin to photograph and document the Jewish factories that served the Third Reich. These news articles were used as propaganda to show the rest of the world how "well" the Germans were treating the Jews. And how grateful the Jews were to the Nazis for giving them such good jobs.

There was another unexpected positive side to these *handverkshtaten*. Sometimes the workers would have conversations with their guards. Occasionally, a guard would request that a special item be made for him, and in return, might warn a worker if the Germans were about to attack the Jews. The workers were able to share information with each other, and eventually, some of them began talking about a revolt. They felt that since the Germans were going to kill all the Jews anyway, at least they would die fighting. And they would make sure some Germans would also die.

Chapter 4

July 1942: *A Surprise Sanctuary*

In the summer of 1942, while we were still in shock, and grieving from the Lida Massacre, a heinous rumor spread like wildfire throughout the ghetto. According to this rumor, while their parents were at work, all the children in the Lida ghetto would soon be forcibly removed from their homes. Then they would be taken away and killed. You can imagine the frenzied reactions of all the parents. What to do?

Thanks to my father's position in the hospital, my parents had already formulated a plan. They sat me down, and in calm voices, explained slowly what was going to happen. I was relieved when they told me that Papa was going to take me with him to the hospital. It would be nice to spend time with him at his job caring for sick and injured people. My relief didn't last long. In fact, I was quickly overcome with misery as my mother told me that I wasn't actually going just to spend time with Papa. Instead, I was going to be admitted as a patient to the hospital! Papa would give me injections that would make me look and feel as if I were very sick. I'd be put in the Infectious Ward with patients who had terrible contagious diseases. This was definitely *not* going to be "nice." Plus, it would put me in the exact situation that had always been my biggest fear: helpless and separated from my parents.

The next day, just as planned, Papa and I walked hand-in-hand through the Nazi-guarded gates of the ghetto, and over to Lida's hospital. Papa told me that I should hold my stomach and act as if I were deathly ill. Given my state of panic, this wasn't difficult. As we approached the hospital, he picked me up and carried me inside. At the receptions desk, he filled out the necessary paper-work, and had me admitted.

Once I got into a bed, Papa gave me several painful shots that would make me even sicker to my stomach than I already was. He told me the medication would make me sleepy, which was a good thing, because as long as I was asleep, I wouldn't be able to talk. That way I couldn't accidentally tell someone something that should be a secret. Papa also insisted that even when I was awake, I should keep my eyes closed and pretend to be asleep. That way no one would be tempted to talk to me.

The major problems with our plan was that I didn't have any symptoms of an actual illness. I didn't have a fever, I wasn't throwing up, and I didn't have diarrhea. So it didn't take long before a suspicious nurse confronted Papa, and asked what my real problem was. Afraid that his improvised answer hadn't convinced her, Papa knew we had little time before she notified the authorities. He had to get me out of the hospital as soon as possible. In preparation for this possibility, Papa had previously made contact with a Polish farm-woman, whose little daughter's life he'd once saved. He'd hoped that the woman would return the favor by saving his daughter's life. He was relieved and grateful when she agreed to take me in, especially since she and her daughter would be executed if caught hiding a Jewish child.

Throughout the next day, Papa would come and pretend to examine me whenever the nurses left the ward. He would whisper encouragement in my ears, and give me little hugs. Finally, Mama came to my room. I could barely contain my delight! She held my hand as Papa quietly told me that I was leaving the hospital immediately with him and Mama. I didn't even have time to get excited or ask questions. Within a few moments, Mama had dressed me, taken my hand, and walked me out of the room, down the hall, out the door, and across the hospital grounds to a small group of trees.

My happiness that the three of us were going home together did not last long. My mother bent over to brush the hair out of my eyes, and spoke softly to me. What she said was beyond my brain's ability to process. Instead of going home, I would be going to live with a widowed Catholic woman and her little daughter on their farm. I desperately clutched Mama's arm, and choked back a gasp of fear. The only time I felt safe was when I was with my parents. What on earth was I going to feel like far away with strangers—in a strange, Catholic home? It didn't take much imagination for me to believe that I'd never see my parents again.

Suddenly, a strange man appeared. He shook hands with Papa and nodded to Mama. Then my parents gave me a small bag of clothes along with my final directions. As I stared at them in disbelief, they told me that my name was no longer Mirele—it was now Mirka. And instead of being Jewish, I was a Polish Catholic girl. I had to erase all knowledge of Jews and Judaism. I must never speak Yiddish. That way no one would suspect that I was a Jew.

If anyone asked, I was the farm woman's recently orphaned niece. I was to obey her at all times, always help her with chores, and keep her little girl entertained. Furthermore, I should be sure not to pester her with a lot of annoying questions, and above all, I should not cry. Ever. Before giving me my last kisses and hugs, Mama and Papa assured me that we would be together again. During this whole time, I couldn't even form words, so I wasn't able to say goodbye to them. I couldn't help but think about the last time I saw my grandparents—and my mother's repeated assurance *then*, that we'd be together again soon.

When the strange man, whose name I never learned, took my hand, I shrank from his rough touch. This was only the second time I'd been touched by a man who wasn't a loving member of my own family. The first was when that German officer picked me up on the street. On both occasions, I was trapped, and had to stifle my instinctive urge to escape. Now, even though I tried to cooperate, my legs refused to move, so the man ended up dragging me along beside him. Thoughts of breaking free and running away evaporated with the ever-tightening grip of his hand. My heart felt like it was going to explode.

I was still sick from Papa's shots. My feet hurt, my hand hurt. My head hurt. It seemed as if everything hurt, but with my parents' directions still ringing in my ears, I refused to let myself cry. I still couldn't talk, so I continued in silence despite the man's attempts to start a conversation. We trudged on for several hours, without eating, drinking, or going to the bathroom. When I think about it now, I'm sure he was as terrified as I was—if not even more so—because he knew that if we were caught, we'd both would be shot.

We finally reached the farm house just as the sun was setting. The farm woman welcomed me warmly, and told her little daughter, Irenka, that I was her cousin, Mirka, and that she now would have someone to play with. She was excited to have a cousin to keep her company while her mother was out in the fields. Just like me, she'd been terrified to stay in the house by herself. To her I was a beloved relative, a big girl she could look up to. This was a new feeling for me. As a seven-year-old, I'd never been a "big girl" to anyone before, so despite my misery at that moment, I felt a bit of pleasure at this new status.

Surprisingly, there would be some other benefits to this strange new living arrangement. The farm woman told me I should call her *Ciocia* (Chio-chia), which means, "Auntie," in Polish. Then she took me to wash up. When I looked and felt a little less like a wild animal and a bit more human, she sat me down at the farm table, and gave me the first real dinner that I could remember. My eyes almost popped out of my head when I saw—and smelled—roasted chicken, fresh vegetables, and warm, just-baked bread. I had to convince myself that this wasn't a dream.

Thinking that my loaded plate must be a platter from which we would each be served, I started to take some food and pass the plate along to her daughter. With a little laugh, Ciocia assured me that I didn't have to share—the plate was all mine and I could eat as much as I wanted! This was a definite improvement over my usual half-bowl of watery soup made from rotten potatoes, and who knows what else. I wonder if she was shocked when I ate every morsel and crumb, and then asked for seconds.

After this splendid meal, Ciocia took my hand and showed me around the house. It had electricity and an indoor bathroom. And then she took me to a bedroom that would be all my own. In it were a chest of drawers, a table, a lamp, and best of all, a beautiful bed, covered with clean, crisp sheets, blankets and a pillow! No one else would be rolling over on me or sleeping on the floor. When I went to bed that first night, my stomach was full, but so was my heart—full of mixed emotions. Exhausted, I immediately fell asleep. And strangely enough, I didn't have any nightmares.

I was awakened at dawn by the unusual sound of a rooster. And I was confused to find myself alone in an actual bed. But most confusing of all, was the long-forgotten, enticing aroma of baking bread and frying eggs that filled my room. I blinked my eyes and tried to make sense of my surroundings. Was I safe? Where were Mama and Papa? Was I having a dream instead of a nightmare?

When I finally realized where I was, and that I was far from my parents, the fear and loneliness I'd been holding in overwhelmed me. I began to sob and shake uncontrollably. It seemed as if every horror of the last year was erupting from my little body, heart, and soul. Emotionally exhausted, I realized that I'd better get control of myself or Ciocia would become alarmed. I also knew that crying not only wouldn't do me any good — it would only make me look weak. My parents had told me to be strong and make them proud of me. Plus, I was really hungry. So I gathered my courage, stood up straight, and went to wash my face.

Determined to look cheerful, I marched into the kitchen, where I saw that the bountiful breakfast I'd been smelling was spread out on the table. Again, I ate like a starved animal who didn't know if and when her next meal would appear. Irenka watched me closely with big eyes—she was as astonished by my appetite as I was by the amount of food on the table! After breakfast, she and I cleaned up the dishes, and then went outside to play. Before leaving to go work in the fields, Ciocia put some bread, cheese, and fruit out for us to eat at lunchtime. When she returned that evening, we ate supper together.

Our days followed the same routine, and even took on a sense of normalcy. In addition to watching out for Irenka, I was eager to help with any household or farm task, and Ciocia let me know she appreciated my help. So I was well-fed, breathing fresh, clean air, contributing to the well-being of the household, and feeling relatively safe. Underlying this sunny surface, however, there was the ever-present darkness of fear.

No matter how much fun we were having, or how deeply I slept, I always had to be careful—especially when visitors came to the house. This was because my dark hair and eyes stood out in stark contrast to those of my blonde, blue-eyed "relatives," and might cause outsiders to question my true identity. The minute I heard other people approach, I would run to my room, where I stayed quietly until they left. When this wasn't possible, I tried to be as inconspicuous as I could. If anyone noticed anything suspicious about me, they would report my presence to the authorities, and Ciocia, Irenka, and I would be executed.

It's hard for a little girl to be constantly vigilant. On one sunny afternoon, when I was lost in thought, I got a painful reminder about paying attention. I hadn't noticed the bee that swooped down and stung the back of my head. I was angry that I hadn't been aware of the danger until it was too late. I didn't complain about the pain because it seemed like a fitting penalty for my inattention. And it taught me that even the sweetest moments can be taken away quickly—and painfully.

My heightened sense of alertness couldn't prevent a bad surprise from coming on the next Sunday morning. Irenka and I were outside when I spotted a neighbor lady enter the front yard. Hoping to avoid her, I scurried into the house and dashed into my room. Unfortunately, I hadn't escaped her notice. But it wasn't because of my dark hair and eyes. It was because Irenka and I were not in church. She was so offended that two little Catholic girls were playing in the yard instead of praying in church, that she insisted on taking us with her with to Mass. Not wanting to make the woman suspicious, Ciocia thanked her with a smile, and quickly combed our hair. We put on clean clothes, and went along with the woman. Irenka kept chattering away and asking me endless questions, and was frustrated that I wouldn't answer her. She didn't know that if the woman heard my accent, she'd know I wasn't Irenka's cousin.

I'd never been in a Catholic church before. Just walking from the bright sunshine and into the dark sanctuary was a shock—as was the sight of so many candles—and I wondered why there was a sad-looking, almost-naked man hanging from a cross! People kept doing strange motions with their hands in front of their chests and faces. There was lots of kneeling, and lots of standing. Somehow despite my fear, and the fact that I couldn't understand a word the priest was saying, I managed to remain alert and observant so that I could copy what the other people were doing. I knelt. I stood up. I crossed myself. I mouthed the words to their songs. And I sat quietly, with my head bowed, pretending to pray—when I was really wondering why all these Catholics were safe, but I was in danger.

I must have behaved appropriately, because I did not arouse any suspicion. And later that week, almost as if it were a reward for my good performance at church, the man who had brought me to the farm, suddenly reappeared. To my delight, he brought me a package from my parents. Inside, there were some satiny blue hair ribbons. More importantly, there was a letter from Mama. Since I was only seven, hadn't ever been to school, and only knew what Mama had taught me, she wrote simple Polish words in large print. I remember them to this day:

> *My Dearest Mireczka, Papa and I are well. We are very busy working. We miss you very much. We are so proud of what a good, brave, big girl you are. We hear that you are a big help to your Aunt. We hope the war is over soon so that we will be together again. Be well, sweet girl, Your loving Mama*

As I read the letter all my bravery vanished. I became completely unglued. I clutched the ribbons in my hand as I lay sobbing and tossing and turning in my bed. Every time I caught my breath, I would reread the letter, and the cycle would begin again. When I'd memorized her words, I would say them aloud, and respond to her as if she could hear me. "Mama, please let me come back to you and Papa. Please let us all die together."

For days I could not be comforted. My pillow never dried, and the pretty ribbons became dirty and wrinkled. The letter became such a wadded-up mess that the words were no longer legible. Ciocia and Irenka worried that I was sick, and tried to cheer me up. But all I could do was stare at them in stony silence. And then, just when I didn't think I could survive my misery, a miracle—at least from my point of view—occurred.

Apparently, the rumor of the impending extermination of all Jewish children in the Lida ghetto had just been the Germans' idea of fun. They enjoyed keeping us all in a state of terror. Feeling that it was safe for me to come back to the ghetto, my parents arranged for the man who'd brought me to the farm to bring me home. Ciocia had kindly offered to keep me, but my parents didn't want to put her and Irenka in any more danger.

I said my goodbyes to my loving Ciocia and little Irenka, who both hugged me with tears in their eyes. Irenka rolled up one of her own pink hair ribbons and put it in my pocket, so I would never forget her. Ciocia packed a basket full of food so we wouldn't be hungry. Of course I didn't know it then, but their kindness to me had put their lives in mortal danger. I also didn't know that I would never see them again.

This time, the several-hour walk was not as difficult—in fact, I practically skipped the whole way! This time, the weather was better, and we had plenty to eat. This time, I wasn't afraid of the man, and I probably wore him out with my constant chattering. This time I wasn't on my way to live in a strange place with strange people—and I wouldn't have to pretend I wasn't a Jew.

We returned to the same cluster of trees outside the hospital where he had picked me up a month before. The man patted me on the top of my head, wished me well—and then left me all by myself. The few minutes I stood there alone felt like forever. My excited anticipation faltered a bit as I began to worry if Papa would come get me. One of my worst nightmares had just come to life: I was all alone, without any resources, and in terrible danger. I pretended to be a statue and practiced not breathing, but eventually, though my body didn't move, I started gasping for air, and I couldn't stop the tears.

At first, they were just a trickle. A little crying statue, standing alone under a tree. Then, just as the tears began to flood out of my eyes, I saw the hospital's side-door open. Papa peeked out and looked around carefully, checking to make sure no one would see us. Then, wearing his white doctor's coat, with his stethoscope hanging from his neck, and his red cross armband, he strode purposefully toward me—motioning with his hand that I should stay just where I was instead of running to meet him. The moment he was close enough to touch me, however, I lost all semblance of self-control. I leapt into his arms, sobbing, heaving, gasping, and clutching him so tightly, that my hands and legs cramped and went numb. My nose started to run and then bleed. Covered with my various bodily fluids, Papa looked like he'd been performing a messy surgery instead of meeting his daughter.

As soon as I could form words, I couldn't stop them. I started begging him to never, ever send me away again. And since he couldn't promise me anything, he just hugged me close, stroked my back, gently cleaned my face and hands with his handkerchief, and set me down on my feet. Holding hands tightly, we walked back to the ghetto as if we'd just taken a little stroll for fresh air. Of course, in the midst of this pleasantness, I was on the alert for Germans. And bees.

The instant my mother came into view, I lost control of my mind and body again. When she bent down to hug me, I held on to her neck so hard, that I'm sure she had trouble breathing. My hysterics made her ask me if I'd been mistreated at the farm. Still unable to speak, I shook my head "no."

I eventually calmed down. But just as I was beginning to feel safe, I was in for yet another bad surprise. As we sat, holding on to each other, Mama sadly told me that Aunt Ala and Uncle Tadek would soon be sneaking out of the ghetto to return to Warsaw. This was beyond my comprehension. Why were they leaving us? How could they leave me? But, as often happens with adults, they had already made their plans without asking for my advice. They were determined to go home to Warsaw, to help my grandparents. Nothing would stop them. My emotions had rapidly bounced from terror, to joy; from security to anxiety; and finally, to utter despair at being abandoned.

Once again I heard those no-longer reassuring words, "Don't worry, we'll all be together soon." By then, however, I realized that these "encouraging" expressions were just words that adults uttered in order to keep children calm in times of danger. Hearing them now just intensified my anxiety.

Years later, I learned that my anxiety had been well-founded. My beloved Aunt Ala and Uncle Tadek did not survive the war. We never learned what had happened to them. Maybe they'd been robbed and killed by the people who had been paid to help them. Or turned over to bounty-hunters. Maybe they'd been caught by Germans on the way. Maybe they'd actually reached Warsaw. Maybe they'd been shot by a trigger-happy Nazi. Or maybe they'd survived all these horrors, only to have been deported to Treblinka and murdered with my Grandparents.

My father, mother, and Aunt Ala in the Lida ghetto: 1942

Chapter 5
November 1942: *Escaping the Lida Ghetto*

The transition from Ciocia's farm—which had been so full of life—back to the ghetto which was so full of death, was a huge shock. The already desperate conditions there had deteriorated even further after the May 8 Massacre, and the once overcrowded ghetto was almost empty. This emptiness would not last long, however, because in their effort to make the entire region Judenfrei, the Germans soon began emptying small towns and cities of their Jews and transporting them to the Lida ghetto.

As thousands of terrified Jews of all ages were forced through our gates, the Lida ghetto became over-crowded again. As this was happening, I absorbed the tension around me, and grew more and more quiet. I also became uncannily alert to even the most minor changes in my parents' moods, and facial expressions, as well as the sounds of their voices.

By now, most of the Jews in the Lida ghetto were so weak mentally and physically, that they couldn't even imagine escaping this nightmare. They were just waiting to die. Looking back, I now understand that in the aftermath of the Massacre, the grief-stricken, sick, and starving survivors had finally realized that the Germans planned to exterminate all of us. And they planned to do it soon.

There were, however, some 120 young Jews who refused to accept this fate. They were hungry, angry, and determined that if they had to die, they would die fighting. They wanted vengeance, and planned to inflict as much damage on the Germans as humanly possible. And while most of these young men

39

and women spoke at least three languages, the word, "mercy," was not in any of their vocabularies.

Now typically, Jewish homes are not training-grounds for hatred and violence. Jewish households usually were filled with books instead of guns. Jewish children were taught to lead lives of *Tikkun Olam*—repairing or healing the world. Jewish teens spent most of their time going to school, working, and studying—not learning how to lie, steal, assemble weapons, blow up train-tracks, and shoot or stab their enemies. They'd never been trained to defend themselves. But somehow, the group of 120 grew quickly, and 300-500 young Jews managed to escape to the Lipiczany and Naliboki forests. And they wasted no time in learning to actively fight the Germans. These heroic warriors who chose to die fighting for freedom instead of being murdered like sheep, would become known as "partisans."[7]

Fortunately for them, they had a strong, resourceful, and talented leader. His name was Boruch Levin. He had miraculously escaped to Lida from his home in a nearby town after a German attack had killed most of the Jews, including his family. An expert mechanic, Levin now inhabited a musty, windowless attic on Kholodna Street in the ghetto. Unbeknownst to all but a few Lida ghetto residents, he had set up his own version of a workshop in his attic room. But instead of making gloves and belts for the Germans, he was making weapons. Working closely with him was a small, but fierce crew of young Jews who were also determined to kill Germans.

Levin's group secretly bought, scavenged, and stole the materials and spare parts they needed to create a weapons arsenal. They met each night, and as they shared information and devised strategies, they also sharpened knives and axes, repaired old guns, and made grenades and bombs. They eventually put together a collection of deadly weapons that would be used by groups of partisans who had set up camps in the forest.

Eventually, their secret leaked out—the way secrets always do—and rumors about the hidden workshop began to spread throughout the ghetto. The reactions to these rumors differed widely. While many of the young people welcomed the opportunity to take a stand and fight the Nazis, some older people were opposed because they felt that their jobs in the workshops would protect them. While the members of the Judenrat were not opposed to a revolt, they didn't want its organizers to be headquartered inside the ghetto. They knew it would be impossible to keep it a secret, and it would only be a matter of time before the Germans heard about it. Their response would be swift and deadly.

---

7 Partisans were secret, illegal, armed freedom fighters who fought fiercely against the Nazis.

Realizing that the Judenrat's concerns were valid, most of the young fighters packed up their supplies and, snuck out of the ghetto. They were enthusiastically welcomed by the partisans in the forest. Despite the danger, however, Boruch Levin needed to stay in the ghetto so that he could recruit and train more Jewish fighters, and coordinate actions with the partisans. He also organized and guided small groups of escapees from the ghetto to partisan camps.

My mother had heard rumors about these partisans at her workshop. At night, she quietly discussed their activities with Papa. While my parents admired the courage of these daring young fighters, they worried about what the Germans would do to the rest of us if these rebels were discovered. Their defiance could cost all of us our lives. To my parents, the very presence of partisans brought mixed feelings. While they were proud of the young Jews who had decided to fight, they also knew that partisan activities would endanger the rest of us. This meant that my parents had one more danger to protect me from—and this time, it came from our own people.

On the night of November 9, 1942, two of the Jewish partisans who had previously escaped the ghetto and joined a partisan group, received important orders from their commandant. They were told to sneak back into the ghetto and bring two important men back to the forest. One of these men was Boruch Levin, whose leadership abilities, mechanical skills, and stock-pile of weapons were now more essential in the forest than in the ghetto. The other man was my father, the renowned surgeon, Dr. Chaim Miasnik, who had his own stockpile of medical supplies and medicines.

The partisans sent Papa a message to meet them that night at a safe-house so they could discuss their plans. When he arrived, they told him he was needed in the forest, and must leave with them immediately. Stunned by this news, Papa explained that he couldn't possibly go with them until he discussed the situation with his wife. When the partisans insisted, Papa refused to discuss the matter any further and came home.

I was awakened by my parents whispered arguments about the dangers of taking a child into the wild forest during winter. Papa wanted to refuse to go with the partisans because he felt it would be too dangerous for us. My mother, however, insisted it was our only chance to survive. She knew that my father could refuse all he wanted, but his refusals wouldn't have any impact on the partisans—they would just go ahead and take him. Left alone with me, Mama would be at the mercy of the Germans who would notice the doctor's absence, and take revenge on us.

After going back and forth about this for quite a while, Papa saw the logic in Mama's argument, and eventually agreed to take us. Now all he had to do was to persuade the partisans to let us come along.

The next morning, Mama explained to me that the three of us would leave the ghetto that night. I asked her if I could tell Tuska, so she wouldn't be scared when she saw that we had left, but Mama said that I absolutely could not tell anyone—*no matter what*. She explained that we would be joining other Jewish fighters at a secret camp in the forest. Papa would provide medical care to these partisans, and Mama and I would help him whenever possible.

Except for my sadness at leaving Tuska, this actually sounded like an adventure to me. So I looked forward to sneaking out of the ghetto, and going to live in freedom with brave Jews who were armed and fighting for all of us. Even though I was only seven, I could see and understand that everyone in the Lida ghetto was marked for death. Besides, what could go wrong as long as my parents were with me?

Before I went to bed that night, Mama helped me put on extra layers of clothing. Later, when the others—including me—had finally fallen asleep, she came and gently placed her hand over my mouth so I wouldn't make any noise. Then she lifted me out of bed, and carried me to the front door. Mama had already packed a suitcase with warm clothes and blankets—including the wonderful down-comforter that had comforted me so many times in my young life. Papa carried a big box of medical supplies that he had snuck out of the hospital.

Without making a sound, we slipped out the door and into the cold, dark, empty street. With Papa going first, and Mama behind me, we walked single-file, staying close to the buildings. Soon, much to my surprise, we stopped in front of a neighbor's house. It looked empty to me, but Papa motioned that we should go inside. In the dimness of a solitary flickering candle, I could barely make out that the front room was filled with people. Our two partisan guides and their leader, Boruch Levin, were among them. I was the only child.

When one of the men came over and ripped the yellow Stars of David off our clothes, I knew for sure that we were really leaving the ghetto. Nearby, I overheard a man ask my father if I was really capable of being part of the group. He wanted to make sure that I could keep up with them and not make any noise. My father assured him that I was exceptionally well-disciplined, ready to follow all orders, and would never cry out. Luckily for me, Papa was highly respected, so his assurances were accepted. Also lucky for me was the chance to hear my father's praise—I hadn't realized that he'd had such a high opinion of me! I vowed to never do anything that would make him regret taking me with him. Covering my mouth with my hand, I risked a small smile, and breathed a long sigh of relief that my worries were finally over.

After midnight, we left the house and silently headed to the barbed-wire fence surrounding the ghetto—not an easy task for a group of 15 terrified people. The men used clippers to make a small opening through which we could crawl. We had to cover our hands and faces with our coats to avoid getting scratched. Then the men rewired the fence so our exit would not be noticed and endanger the Jews who remained behind.

Continuing in silence, we walked like ghosts along the Lideika River, which still flowed unfrozen in the winter darkness. I felt a funny flutter in my stomach when I looked at the lighted windows of apartment buildings in the distance. I knew those apartments, now occupied by Germans, had once been homes to Jewish families.

With every step, I became more and more anxious, and just when I thought I couldn't contain my fear any longer, my worst fears were realized. Gunshots pierced the quiet night. Everyone in the group flinched and then looked toward our leaders for directions. Without a word they each pointed to the river. We understood that we would have to go into the cold water. We waded in far enough so we could bend down, keeping all but our heads below the surface. Terrified that we had been spotted, we waited until the shooting stopped. Then, soaked and freezing, we eased our way out of the water and continued our journey. Even if we'd been allowed to talk, our shivering bodies and chattering teeth would have made speaking impossible.

And it wasn't just being cold and wet that made us shiver. We were in constant danger of being detected by dogs whose barking would alert Germans. And they weren't our only enemies. Many of the Polish citizens of Lida collaborated with the Germans, and either turned Jews in for rewards, or shot them on the spot. So anyone peeking out a window, presented deadly danger to us. Even in the darkness, I could tell by the way the adults slowed their pace, that their anxiety level had suddenly increased. The reason soon became clear to me.

Instead of continuing to follow the river toward the forest and freedom, as we'd expected, we'd been motioned to go the other way. We were confused by the direction to follow the river toward the center of Lida. This meant that we would be walking straight toward the area where the Germans now lived— some of them in those apartments that had once been Jewish homes. We could feel each other's terror as we walked toward what we thought would mean our certain deaths.

Papa quietly asked one why we were going deeper into town instead of escaping out of it, but much to his frustration, he received no answer. Our lives were now in the hands of the leaders, and we couldn't turn back. In a snowy field near the center of town, our leader suddenly held up his hand, signaling us to stop at a small hill.

In this night of utter confusion, I couldn't imagine why we were stopping in this field. I became even more confused when I saw several of the men pull shovels out of their packs, and begin digging furiously through the snow to the dirt below. What on earth could this mean? All I could think was that they were digging holes for us to hide in—or to be buried in—neither of which I wanted to do!

My confusion cleared when I saw the men lift bundles from the holes in the ground. Much to my surprise, these bundles contained machine guns and ammunition that had been hidden by Soviet soldiers when they'd fled the Nazi invasion of Lida. A local communist who had known about the hidden weapons, had given this information to the partisans. Now we understood why we first had to walk deeper into Lida instead of going straight to the forest! After the men filled-in the holes, covered them with snow, and brushed away any evidence of our activities, we finally began our journey out of Lida.

It had been hours since we'd left the ghetto. And even though we'd reached the countryside, we still couldn't talk or make any noise, because every farm had dogs who would bark furiously at any sign of a human. I was proud that so far, I had kept up with the adults, and that Papa hadn't had to carry me. I was, however, on the brink of total exhaustion. Just as dawn broke, when I was afraid I wouldn't be able to take another step, our group came to a farm house. This time, instead of sneaking past it, our leaders motioned that we should go inside.

Luckily for us, the farmer was a good man who supported the partisans, and had agreed to take us all in. He told us to sit by the warm fireplace, and provided us with clean clothes and food. We undressed and hung our wet things up to dry. After a quick meal, we collapsed on the floor and slept. Snuggled in between Mama and Papa, I felt safe and secure in our little family nest.

After just a few hours, the farmer woke us up and fed us a wonderful breakfast of freshly baked bread, cheese, and Russian tea. Warmly dressed and energized by our full bellies, we set out in the bright winter sunshine full of hope for the rest of our journey to the partisan camp. It didn't take long for us to be confronted with a challenge. We had to cross the partially frozen Niemen River. We slogged through the frigid shallow water before slipping and falling in an unexpectedly deeper section. In one expanse of water that was too deep for me to navigate, Boruch Levin carried me on his back.

We emerged from the water, soaked through to our skins and shivering with cold. I couldn't feel my fingers, my toes, or my nose. I was even too cold to feel my growing hunger pangs. We trudged on, however, confident in the expert guidance of Boruch Levin. When we finally entered the Lipiczany forest, it was as if someone had turned out the lights. The dense, interlocking canopies of tree branches crowded out almost every trace of the sky and the sun. Even when we could see where we were going, there were no paths to follow. Unexpected patches of ice caused us to slip and fall, making our way even more treacherous, Adding to the strangeness of this new environment was the thick fog that rose from the undergrowth, and seemed to swallow everything in its path—including us.

Sometimes our progress was stopped by vast stretches of ice-covered swamps, which we either had to carefully walk over or around. This added extra hours to our journey, and increased our exhaustion. As frightening as this strange forest-world was, it actually helped us because the Germans avoided it at all costs. They got lost easily, and since they couldn't bring in their vehicles, they were out in the open and provided easy targets for partisans.

After so many hours of enforced silence, my curiosity bubbled up and I couldn't help asking Papa, "How do the men know where to go?" Instead of answering me, he whispered that I should be quiet and continue following the others. Which is exactly what I did for I don't know how many hours. Just when I felt as if I couldn't continue standing for another minute, much less taking another step, it appeared that I wouldn't have to — we had finally reached our destination! We were alive! We were safe!

Chapter 6
December 1942: *The Jewish Partisans*

The fire, whose flickering we had occasionally spied earlier in the forest, welcomed us as we stepped out of the darkness and into the cleared campsite. The joyful partisans, most of whom knew my parents, welcomed us with hugs and congratulations. They also welcomed us with a wonderful hot meal of meat and potatoes, which we ate greedily—and gratefully!

As I gradually adjusted to my surroundings, I became aware that all conversations were being conducted in Yiddish—with a little Polish and Russian thrown in. What a comfort and joy it was to be surrounded by Jews who were capable, healthy, and proud. They were not cowering slaves who worked for oppressive masters. They were not brutalized victims dying painfully in a ghetto. These powerful Jews worked together to save Jewish lives. And they worked together to destroy Germans. I could feel the strength, the pride, the skill, and determination of these unbowed Jews, and for the first—but definitely not the last—time in my life, an energizing wave of Jewish pride surged within me.

Except for the immediate area around the fire, all was in darkness. It felt as if we were in a large room, with tall black walls, whose only light was the camp-fire in the middle of the dirt floor. I marveled that all these partisans had managed to succeed in making their way out of the ghettos through the tangled branches and dense underbrush to get to this hidden camp.

Just as I was wondering where we were going to sleep, one of the partisans came over and led us to our new—and very surprising—sleeping quarters. In the darkness, he seemed to be brushing off the snow and lifting branches up from a cave. We could just barely make out the outline of a small opening into what at first looked like a hidden cave. Instead, it was the entrance to an underground bunker.

The partisan motioned us to crawl through this opening. Papa went first, and then caught me as I came through. Then we both helped Mama. It turned out that we had entered what would be our new home. And I learned a new word: *zemlyanka* (ZEM-lee-AN-ka). This underground bunker where we would be living was called a zemlyanka.

Once we settled ourselves on the floor I was pleased with my new-found advantage over my parents: they were too tall to stand up, but I was the perfect size! The dirt floor, the walls, and ceiling were lined with logs that helped provide insulation from the endlessly frigid winter weather, when the temperatures often went down to 45 degrees below zero. We were lucky to also have a small fire on the ground that helped to keep us warm. The smoke was vented to the outside through a hole in the ceiling.

Along the sides of this dug-out, and placed about half-way between the floor and ceiling, platforms of wooden logs served as our beds. Underneath these logs we placed what few clothes we'd been able to bring with us. In the remaining space, there was just barely enough room for the three of us, and while the lack of space made it difficult to move around, the closeness of our bodies helped keep us warm. The upper 1/2 of our new home was built above the ground, and was camouflaged by logs, branches, and ground-cover in summer, and snow in winter.

We fell asleep that first night feeling warm, well-fed, safe, and for the first time in my memory—free and hopeful, surrounded by brave, strong Jews! The next morning, we woke up hungry, and Papa climbed out of the zemlyanka to go ask about breakfast. He came back to let us know that not only was it time to eat, but that pancakes were on the menu! When I asked Mama where all this wonderful food had come from, she pointed out that every partisan was carrying a gun. One of the jobs for partisans was finding food, clothing, medicines and weapons. Raiding farms and nearby villages was the partisan version of going to a market! We would soon learn that there were two kinds of farmers: some were good Communists and supported the partisans, while others collaborated with the Nazis and were hostile to the partisans. In their search for food and warm clothing, the partisans raided only those farmers who were pro-German.

After breakfast, Mama and I helped clean up the eating area, and then stepped a few yards outside of the camp to gather small branches to make fires. Naturally watchful, I made a point of observing my surroundings and the people in them. Something seemed strange, but I couldn't figure out what it was.

Then it dawned on me: I was the only child in the group. I was overwhelmed by horror and sorrow at what must have happened to the children left behind in the ghetto. And I was stunned by how lucky I was that the partisans had allowed my parents to bring me with them.

Mama and I were grateful to be part of this partisan group, and eager to contribute to everyone's well-being. As the newest members, our first assignments related to ensuring basic survival in a forest camp. Mama helped cook, and we both helped serve the food and then clean up. We also scooped snow into big pots, and then melted and boiled it to use for drinking, bathing, and washing laundry. Merciless as the winter was, it did provide plenty of snow—and that provided us with plenty of water. Our days began to take on a predictable routine, and I was proud to be entrusted with these important tasks. Having a schedule and responsibilities created a sense of control and safety. Unfortunately, this would not last long.

The first shock to my sense of safety came within a few days of our arrival. Papa was given orders to leave our camp and travel throughout the forest to other camps, treating wounded and sick partisans. This assignment was the beginning of his regular routine, and we never knew where he was or when he would return. Mama and I hadn't anticipated that we would be on our own so much. Without Papa's presence, we knew we weren't particularly welcome at the camp.

Our second big shock hit us around the third week of December, while Papa was away. Our peaceful existence was utterly shattered when German troops charged into the forest on a three-week rampage killing every Jewish partisan they could find. This was in retaliation for previous partisan raids, where there had been heavy German casualties. Hundreds of non-combat Jews living in family camps, and dozens of partisans—including important leaders—were killed. A courier brought news of this massive attack, and there were immediate, and profoundly shocking consequences for Mama and me.

Without saying a word to us, the inhabitants of our camp packed up and began to leave. We begged them to take us along but they refused because they were afraid a child would increase their risk of getting caught. In disbelief, we watched as the partisans who just minutes before had been going about their daily routines, ran off in different directions. None of them even glanced our way, and before our eyes, the camp became a ghost-town. I understood that there wasn't time for any explanations from Mama, so I held back from asking questions, and just followed her footsteps. She grabbed our few belongings—and me—and we rushed away from the camp. We were completely on our own.

Several days later we ran into a different group of partisans, but they also refused our request to join them. No matter what Mama said, they told her that they absolutely wouldn't take a child—any child—even famous Dr. Miasnik's child. "We can't take the chance of her crying out and giving away our location, we'd all be killed." Mama and I realized that unless Papa was with us, we had no value. I finally understood why there were no other young children allowed in the partisans. And worst of all, I understood that my very existence had become dangerous for my mother.

After scrambling around through the trees and brush for a couple of hours, Mama and I finally caught up with a small rag-tag group of other stragglers. They were as tired, frightened and confused as we were. Maybe that's why they didn't chase us away. After walking with them for what seemed like hours, we could tell that this long devastating day was drawing to a close because the temperatures plunged from being merely bitterly cold to being dangerously frigid. That night, with all of us desperately needing sleep, the group decided to take shelter under the protective bottom branches of a huge spruce tree. Two people volunteered to stand guard so the rest of us could get some sleep. Wrapped tightly in Mama's comforter, Mama and I took turns sleeping. We were terrified that if we both fell asleep, we would freeze to death—or be left behind.

All too soon we were jolted awake by noises about a hundred yards away. It sounded like footsteps were coming toward us through the forest's under-growth. As the footsteps came closer, we began to hear the deep voices of men speaking German. At first I thought I was having a nightmare, but then I heard one of them laugh as if someone had told a funny joke. Holding tightly to each other, and shaking from head to toe, Mama and I could hear each other's hearts pounding. I buried my head in her chest, hoping to shut out the dangers of the night. We had been so brave, suffered and survived so much that the realization that we were about to die just didn't make sense to me.

All I could think about was how Papa would feel when he got back to the camp and saw that everyone was gone. Of course, his heart would be broken. And of course, despite the dangers, he would leave the partisans to try to find us. I knew he would never give up. But I also feared he would never find us alive.

Then, in the midst of these thoughts, as sometimes happens in the worst of situations, we suddenly had some unexpected good luck. It was because there was no moon that night, and the forest was even darker than usual. Thick, black ink dark. It was impossible to see even two feet away. If the Germans had come any earlier, there might have been just enough light to detect our footprints in the snow. Now they couldn't see us even if they were standing three feet away from us—which they soon were. Even more lucky for us was that the soldiers had not brought their attack dogs. The dogs wouldn't have been the least bothered by the darkness, and they would have easily sniffed us out. At best, we would have been discovered and shot. At worst, we would have been torn to shreds by the murderous dogs.

We all held our breaths, hoping not to cough or sneeze. The Germans came closer and closer—we could smell their cigarettes—and their sweat. And then . . . and then . . . they were close enough for us to touch. And they walked right by us. The only sound to be heard was the collective exhalation of our little group. Mama and I stayed right where we were all night, holding each other close, rubbing each other's hands and feet, shaking and shivering in the bitingly cold air. The deathly silence of that long, terrible night, was interrupted only by the occasional howl of a wolf.

At daybreak, it was our turn to keep watch while the others slept. We scooped up some snow to eat for breakfast. When the others awoke, we all began the endless hours, that became endless days, of aimlessly trudging through the underbrush and snow. Exhausted, cold, hungry, and frightened, each step we took was a challenge—especially so because our shoes had worn out long before, and we had to stuff them with frozen leaves. We knew that if we stopped moving, even for a few minutes, we would get frostbitten, lose blood circulation, and then freeze to death.

I was only seven years old, but I had grown up pretty fast, in fact, after age four, I never was a child again. I understood that my survival depended on my mother's survival. Even though she was incredibly strong, and determined not to seem weak in front of me, sometimes exhaustion overpowered her. When that happened, I did my best to appear strong, to cheer her up and urge her on. More important, was what I *didn't* do. I didn't pester her with questions. I realized by then that she didn't have any answers, and I didn't want to make her feel even worse. So I limited my talking to words of encouragement. "*Mamele*," I said in my most grown-up voice, "We have to keep on walking. Don't worry, we'll find the partisans again." She kept my spirits up by telling me how brave I was, and how proud she was of me, and about the wonderful things our family would do together after the war.

Chapter 7

January- February 1943: *The Soviet Partisans*

One night, after being on our own for almost a week, we ran into a group of heavily armed Soviet partisans. "Look, Mama! We did it! We found the partisans! Now we're safe again!" Without looking at me, Mama just shook her head and sadly responded, "I don't know, Mirele. I don't know what to believe anymore." The suddenly defeated tone in her voice worried me, so I worked even harder to be strong. I didn't want another group of partisans to send us away just because I was a child.

Apparently, it was our lucky day, because the Soviets allowed us to stay, and directed us to join them for the night in an old, abandoned zemlyanka. This bunker was larger than the one Mama, Papa, and I had shared at the previous camp, and this time, we'd be sharing it with the partisans. The temperature was way below freezing, and the only way to get warm was to lay down sideways like packed sardines, each person positioned closely against another, so we could share our body-heat. Mama and I hadn't slept soundly for over a week, so even the discomfort, the rancid smells, and the disruptive noises didn't keep us from immediately falling asleep.

The next morning, rested, but hungry, we again ate snow for breakfast. I was so cold that I tried to warm up by running faster to the head of the line, leaving Mama further behind. Because visibility was so limited, neither one of us could have known that while we were walking, the line had split into two parts, each going a different direction. At a clearing, I turned to wave to Mama. Imagine my shock that she was nowhere to be seen. It became apparent that Mama was no longer with us. Or with me. Not only was she gone, but I was alone with four armed men. I felt like my heart, my head, and my stomach would explode in fear.

When these four big, strong, combat fighters saw that a child was tagging along with them, they walked faster so they could leave me behind. Somehow, I made myself run as fast as my little legs could go. With very little breath or voice, I called out to them, begging them not to leave me. I tried whatever I could think of. "Please slow down— please take me with you! Please don't leave me behind to die! I'll do whatever you ask! My Mama went with the others—she'll catch up with us soon! My father is Dr. Miasnik, the forest surgeon. Please take me!"

They ignored me.

But at least they didn't run. All day long, cold, hungry, and out of breath I ran and ran some more—desperately trying to keep those big, strong, combat fighters in sight. They walked just fast enough that I couldn't quite keep up. Perhaps some long-buried sense of decency prevented them from running away. Maybe they had children of their own. The fact that they just walked fast, allowed me to run after them. When I saw this, I stopped wasting my limited energy on trying to get their attention, and focused instead on keeping up with them. If I'd fallen down, I would have died by freezing to death, just as I'd always feared, alone, and unprotected.

Eventually, the men reached a clearing and stopped. I was surprised that the clearing actually looked familiar to me. Imagine my further surprise when I realized that we had arrived at our first camp. Mama's group had gotten there earlier, and she seemed to fly right over the campfire to scoop me up and hold me breathless and spasming in her arms. Sobbing, we clung together, unable to give voice to our joy and relief. We had each spent hours thinking we'd never see each other again. Somehow our joy even overshadowed our severe hunger. We returned to our zemlyanka, and slept in each other's loving and grateful embrace. We were safe—at least for the night.

After two days of rest and recuperation with the partisans, Mama and I awoke and found that they had cleared out, leaving us behind with several other unarmed and unwanted Jews. Without food or protection, we all were at the mercy of any person or any animal roaming through the forest. The zemlyanka wouldn't protect us from anything other than the cold. We had to risk setting out into the forest to find anyone who would take us along.

Strengthened by having found each other, Mama and I set out that very night—with absolutely no idea where we were going or what might happen to us.

We wandered for a few days, constantly battling fear, hunger and the cold, without finding anyone who we might join up with. Every once in a while, the moon and stars would break through the darkness, and we would stop and gaze at the night-time sky. Whenever I saw any stars, whose unexpected normal presence would contrast so starkly with our surreal existence, I wondered if we would ever have normal lives again. Lives where seeing the moon and stars at night would not be so other-worldly. Lives where sunshine would be a normal occurrence. And food. A life where there would be food. *Lots* of food.

We weren't always totally alone. Once in a while, a solitary traveler would cross our path. Sometimes it was a Jew, who was running away from danger, and hoping to find a camp to join. Sometimes it was another lost soul who was hoping to find anyone to travel with. Sometimes it was a partisan courier whose mission was to take important information from one camp to another.

After almost three weeks, one such partisan courier emerged from the forest and stopped to share some of his food, and talk with us. Under other circumstances, it could have been a picnic! We gobbled up the food and enjoyed having friendly, interesting conversation. Soon, the conversation got even better. It turned out that he knew Papa, and had been at a camp with him recently. He remembered Papa telling everyone at the camp that wherever they went into the woods, if they found Mama and me, they should immediately bring us straight to him. Hearing this, Mama and I felt like dancing! How could this have happened? One minute we're wandering around the forest, lost, hungry, and helpless, and the next minute someone appears to take us to Papa! What is also amazing is that it turned out that Papa wasn't even so far away! Now we walked with a bit of a spring in our step, and happily found Papa's camp before nightfall.

All these years later, I can close my eyes, and I instantly become that hungry, cold, dirty, scared but determined, little seven-year old girl again. I remember Papa's face when he saw us—a mixture of joy, agony, and relief. How a man, who wasn't very tall, could encircle both Mama and me in a glorious bear hug, I'll never know. It was as if his arms just kept stretching bigger and bigger right along with the emotions he was feeling.

We probably would have stayed in that hug forever, if Papa hadn't thought to ask us if we were hungry. What a question! He immediately took us from the partisan camp to a nearby Jewish family camp, where 20 people had been living. They were kind to us, and shared their food. We greedily devoured our first cooked meal in weeks. Who knew that potatoes could be such a delicacy? Later, as we lay close together near a small, warm fire, it didn't take long for me to feel safe again. In fact, I felt safe enough to fall into a happy, deep, sleep. I was lucky that I was too young to know that happiness and safety are temporary . . . and very fragile.

The other campers helped us recover from our weeks of cold and hunger. We adjusted to the camp's routines, and shared responsibilities, and actually felt a sense of joy that we were so comfortable. Not being in constant danger, however, soon allowed us to start noticing how truly miserable our living conditions really were.

Our shoes were falling apart, so we wrapped our feet in rags before putting on what was left of our them. But we had a much bigger problem than our shoes: Lice. They covered us from head to toe. They bit constantly and moved from one person to the next, carrying diseases such as typhus. This hideous disease had killed many people in the ghettos, but was even worse in the forest where we had no reliable source of water and no way to clean ourselves. In an effort to get rid of the lice, we would stand half-naked in the snow, and squash them one at a time between our finger-nails, and flick them away. Mama and I would go after the lice on each other's backs and heads. In a day or so, our temporary relief would end as the next batch of lice hatched and took up residence on our bodies.

In addition to dealing with the lice and typhus, we were always hungry. Food was scarce, usually just rotting potatoes and onions. On the rare occasions that we had some flour, we made a kind of potato pancake. Papa brought food when he came to visit us, and sometimes, passing partisans who had raided farms, were generous enough to share. Our misery was compounded by the stress of being constantly on the alert for bounty-hunters. These monsters actually made their living by roaming through the woods and finding Jews to either kill or turn in for a reward. Even a little Jewish girl—alive or dead—would bring a reward. We lived an hour-by-hour, day-to-day existence.

The Germans finally left the forest, and Papa visited us whenever he could, bringing news, and encouragement, in addition to food. Each time he left, I was overcome with dread that disaster would strike. One morning, it did. I awoke to the almost inhuman sounds of my mother coughing and gasping for air. It was as if her lungs would break. She also clutched her stomach in agonizing pain. My worst fear had come true.

I gently lifted her shirt, and began trembling in despair when I saw the hideous red rash on her chest. Even at age seven, I knew the symptoms of deadly typhus, and my heart stood still. With tears streaming down my face, I climbed out of the zemlyanka, and approached a woman in our group who had been kind to us. Begging her to help, I grasped her hand and we hurried back to Mama.

The woman knew exactly what to do. She spoke soothingly to Mama, and placed cold compresses on her face and body to bring the fever down. She tried feeding Mama some soup, but Mama wasn't able to swallow. Between her fever, sweats, and vomiting, she was dangerously close to being dehydrated—which would give the disease even more power.

Mama's condition rapidly worsened, and I hated feeling helpless. I desperately wanted to kiss her, to change her compresses, and to plead with her not to leave me. But I'd been directed to keep a distance, so I wouldn't also catch this dread disease. From my little log bed, three feet away, I watched her with great intensity, hoping that the strength of my gaze could flow into her body.

My anguish at her suffering and my inability to help her were now compounded by a paralyzing terror: My beloved Mama was being taken away from me, and I would be left alone. It had been made crystal clear many times, that no one wanted a little girl hanging around. I knew they wouldn't kick me out of the camp because they needed the food that Papa brought, but I'd be there on my own. No one would actually take care of me. No one could afford to take on the extra responsibility of someone else's child. How could an almost-eight-year-old survive alone against an enemy that was determined to eliminate every Jew from the face of the earth? I couldn't help but wonder why Papa was always somewhere else when we needed him most. Of course I knew how important his work was, but I couldn't help wishing that I could be important, too.

It's amazing how in the middle of an almost impassable forest, when we had no access to telephones or radios—and certainly couldn't email or text each other—that somehow, news still traveled fast. While I was desperately trying to keep Mama alive, and agonizing over my own nonexistent future, Papa was in a distant part of the forest, meeting with a group of partisans. A Jewish courier rushed into the camp and interrupted the meeting, breathlessly demanding of Papa, "Doctor, why are you here when your wife is dying of typhus?" Papa instantly ended the meeting, grabbed several sacks of potatoes, and rushed back through the forest to our camp. When he entered our zemlyanka, I jumped into his arms, trying to explain what was happening and how frightened I was. He held me tight with one arm and bent over Mama, kissed her and smoothed her damp hair.

Tears sprang to his eyes, his body sagged, and then his spirit seemed to die. He set me down gently, and told me to keep watching her. Then, in an effort to hide his fear and sorrow from me, he left the zemlyanka for a few minutes. When I peeked out to see where he was going, I saw my strong, fearless father leaning against a tree, quietly weeping. This powerful, unstoppable man who'd defied every obstacle thrown into his path, this famous physician who'd saved so many others, felt powerless to save the most important person in his world. Seeing Papa this way was a shock beyond anything I'd yet experienced. Throughout my short life, and the harrowing ordeals we managed to survive, my unshakable belief in his ability to protect us had given me confidence to stay strong. It looked as if my unbreakable father was breaking—right before my eyes. And if even the famous Dr. Miasnik couldn't help Mama, then there was no hope.

Papa soon straightened up and wiped his eyes. He came back inside and set about trying to heal his beloved wife. He stayed next to her for five days and nights, trying to drip liquids between her parched lips. He injected Mama with the medications he'd brought, but nothing seemed to help. She continued to lay there, ghostlike, on her wooden-log bed, covered by her now-raggedy, goose-down comforter. Her fever rose, and she drifted in and out of consciousness for almost a week. All Papa could do was try to make her comfortable. It wasn't long, however, before she fell into a coma—the last stage before death. Papa and I looked at each other in despair, knowing that we were losing her. And without Mama, we'd both be lost.

My terror had consumed me and despite being ordered to stay away, I now lay down with Mama, begging her not to leave me. I hoped that I could catch typhus and die with her. The night dragged on in fearful anticipation of her death. Exhausted, I kept drifting off to sleep, and then would jolt awake in fear that she had died. Papa's worn out body gave him no choice but to sleep.

He and I both awoke in the dim light that filtered in at daybreak. I peeked cautiously Mama, expecting the worst—and then glanced at Papa. And he was looking at me! Mama was alive! Not only alive, but smiling at us! And then—the unbelievable happened: she whispered, "Mirele, my Mirele." Her fever had broken! We sat with her the rest of the day, holding teaspoons of liquid to her dry lips, trying to keep her cheered up by telling her how much we loved her.

I didn't learn until many years later that Papa had been worried that the prolonged fever and coma might have damaged her brain. All I knew at that moment was that he asked her to sing a song—which I thought was strange, considering her condition. Much to our relief and delight, Mama came through Papa's little test with flying colors! She held my hand and looked into my eyes, cleared her throat, and then sang—without a single mistake—the same song that had brought me comfort in what then seemed like some other girl's life, "I Know a Little Street in Barcelona."

Never had a song been sung so sweetly—or to a more adoring audience. With tears rolling down our faces, we held our breaths to the very last note. Then

Papa held Mama's face in both hands, kissed her, told her we loved her, and that she would soon be well. I went to share the wonderful news. Everyone in the camp was happy for us. That night we celebrated our good fortune by feasting on potato pancakes, and singing joyful songs—made even more joyful with Mama's precious voice.

Unfortunately, as had happened so many times before, our joy would not last long. In just a few days, a partisan rushed to our camp with the terrible news that some German soldiers had attacked another camp. Papa would have to leave us to go help the injured partisans. This time, our goodbyes felt very strange. "Good-bye" no longer had any meaning. We had no idea where he was going, how long he'd be away, or what kind of dangers he'd be forced to endure. Mama and I knew all too well that we could end up stranded by ourselves again in the forest. Every "leaving" could be forever. Every separation could bring a disaster.

For once, our separation was short. And there was good news. When Papa returned he told us that since the Germans had gone, he could stay with us for a while! Within a few days, our lives seemed to take on a routine. And with routine, came a sense of normalcy—even amidst our utterly abnormal circumstances. I would get up as soon as the morning light crept through the zemlyanka's sheet-covered doorway. Papa would go out first to make sure all was safe. Mama and I would get up and join the others making breakfast. Papa would provide whatever medical care that was needed in our family camp. Sometimes he would have to leave for a few days in order to visit partisan groups that were further away, but these were not long separations. It wasn't wonderful, but at least there weren't any bad surprises. For me, a couple days without a bad surprise meant that the worst was over. I began to relax a bit. I was still too little to understand the big picture: The Germans would never give up their mission to leave no Jew alive.

Sadly, I learned all too quickly that the worst was not over. Just as we were getting used to being a family again, and breathing more easily, a courier arrived with an urgent message for Papa. I saw the expression on my father's face change from calm to shocked. He sadly told us that he had to leave immediately to take care of some severely wounded partisans in another part of the forest. And that he would be gone for a long time.

Chapter 8

February —May 1944: *The Forest Hospital*

All those times that Papa had been away from us, all those times when we felt abandoned, he had been taking desperately needed medical care to the partisans. And he was completely alone. In addition to constantly worrying about Mama and me, he had to worry about Germans, bounty-hunters, and the weather. He also faced terrible challenges in finding and treating patients. I'm still amazed when I think about what he achieved under such appalling conditions.

The most frustrating of these occurred when the survival of an injured fighter depended on his receiving fast treatment. "Fast treatment" was not possible in the forest—even "slow treatment" was a challenge. This was because the forest was massive, the weather was oppressive, danger from Germans a constant threat, and, of course, transportation was non-existent. So he could only go as fast as he could walk—while carrying medical supplies, which included a container of boiled water, another of rubbing alcohol to disinfect his hands and the patient's wounds, and a bag of boiled surgical instruments and cloths. He also carried a bottle of vodka to dull his patients' pain since there was no anesthetic.

Just finding the patient in time was difficult. This was because Papa had to depend on directions provided by a partisan courier, who had probably seen the patient at least a day earlier, before trying to track Papa down wherever he might be. Adding to these difficulties were frequent weather changes that affected the directions. A heavy rain, for example, could flood areas, making them impassible, forcing him to make time-consuming detours. All too often, by the time Papa finally arrived, the patient had already died. If not, Papa treated patients and performed whatever surgery he could—outdoors, on the forest floor, in all kinds of weather, amidst buggy, leech-infested swamps, during the summers—and on snow and ice in the winters.

Seriously sick or injured partisans could not be moved, so after they'd received Papa's care, they had to fend for themselves—with whatever food, bandages, and medicine that he could leave with them. After each procedure, Papa had to quickly move on to another part of the forest to help yet another casualty. After all the effort he put in to helping his patients, he sadly realized that few of them would even survive their injuries—much less find their way back to their partisan group.

It became obvious that bringing medical care to patients throughout the forest was not effective. The constant travel was exhausting, Papa desperately needed assistants, and his patients needed care during their recovery. He knew that the only way to provide adequate care was for patients to be placed in a clean, well-supplied, professionally functioning hospital. Of course he also knew this was not possible. Even so, an idea had begun to develop in his mind. And with every frustrating mission to find and care for a patient, the idea grew more and more powerful.

Soon, what had begun as an impossible wish, became a definite goal. Papa decided to make the hospital in the forest a reality. And he planned to get the Soviets to help make the impossible happen. Of course, once Papa made his mind up, nothing could stop him. He used all his persuasion skills with the Soviet forest leaders. Eventually, after going back and forth about the details, the Soviet forest commander agreed to Papa's plan--and they didn't waste any time getting started. Papa, along with an additional recently-arrived Jewish doctor, and a powerful partisan from the Russian command, immediately set out to scout for a possible location. They were gone for several days.

After searching through the forest, and finding something wrong with every potential spot—it wasn't hidden well enough, there wasn't a nearby source of water, it was too close to partisan camps, it was too far from partisan camps, it was too easy to access, it was too difficult to access—they finally agreed on a small island in the middle of a vast cluster of swamps. This location probably would not at first seem like an ideal choice for a medical care facility. Considering, however, that it was remote from the Germans, and access to it was moderately difficult, it actually was ideal.

To further guarantee that the hospital and its whereabouts would remain secret, the group agreed that no one, other than those directly involved in medical care, along with the leaders of each partisan group, would ever be told its whereabouts. Furthermore, partisan guards would be stationed at the sole entry point to the island, and anyone who wanted to get near the hospital had to know the secret password to get past these guards.

There was no time to waste, so as soon as the location was determined, the building process began. Imagine building a hospital on an island in the middle of a swamp without construction materials or machines. Plus, how were people supposed to get across the swamp to access the island? Building a bridge was impossible. Even if they could build one, they would just have had to dismantle it when the hospital construction was completed, so that the Germans couldn't use it. So what do you think they decided to do?

As usual, they worked with what they had. And what they had were floating logs—narrow, unstable, slippery, splintery, moldy, rotting, floating logs that were covered with slimy, blood-sucking leeches. Needless to say, everyone quickly became experts in crossing these precarious log bridges. Well, almost everyone. Those who didn't, were "rewarded" with extremely unpleasant, stinky, swamp baths, leeches all over their faces and bodies—and an occasional outburst of laughter from onlookers—before being rescued. Very soon, these stalwart, resourceful Jewish escapees from the horrors of the Nazis, added the ability to "walk on water" to their collection of other survival skills.

Mama and I moved to the island before the hospital was completed so we could help Papa set up what would be his surgery center. Even before it was all set up, patients began to arrive at the entrance to the swamp. Sometimes they limped in alone, and sometimes they were carried by other partisans. Once the password was accepted by the guards, the patient would be carried across the swamp on the floating log "bridge." This was a complicated process. Two "stretcher-bearers" would carefully put the patient on a stretcher and then lift it. Holding the stretcher between them, they would cautiously step onto an unstable, log. Once they felt stable enough, they then would step onto another, and another, until they reached the island. When a stretcher wasn't available, a wounded partisan was carried across on a scuffling partisan's back.

Our day-to-day activities were simple, and revolved around both our own survival and providing medical care for others. The hospital camp looked like other camps in the forest, and no one could tell what was going on within it. There were two large, carefully camouflaged zemlyankas. All 30 of us slept together in one of them. The other was the actual surgical center.

Two additional Jewish doctors and three Jewish nurses soon came to be part of the medical staff. The rest of us helped in any way we could. We sterilized surgical instruments by putting them in pots to boil over the fire. Meals were cooked by two women, also over an open fire, and we all ate outside—even in the worst weather. Whenever possible, a group of partisans would go on midnight missions to raid hospitals in nearby towns for surgical instruments as well as medical supplies. Non-medical staff raided nearby farms for food and clothing.

Once we were settled in a reasonably safe location that was guarded by highly trained partisans, I began to breathe a little more easily. It was ironic that being surrounded by murky swamps in the middle of the wilderness gave me the first sense of safety that I could remember. And for the first time in two months, it looked as if we would be able to stay in one place until the war ended.

Even in the midst of our new-found safety, however, it turned out that there actually was a danger I'd never even thought of. Thank goodness that Papa and Mama did. They realized that a fully functioning hospital community would be bringing strangers into our midst—strangers who might be a danger to a little girl. So my parents decided I'd be safer if I looked like a boy. Papa first cut my hair and then shaved my head, which felt weird. Mama sewed military-style boys' clothing for me to wear—which I liked because I thought it made me look older, and important! Luckily, I was very adaptable—I'd already changed from Jewish to Catholic, and then back to Jewish—and so changing into boy felt like an adventure.

For reasons I didn't understand then, being a boy felt much more power-ful than being a girl—and I enjoyed it! I was especially proud one afternoon, when a big, tough, partisan shook my hand and told me, "Now you look like a real partisan, Mirka." Determined to act like a boy, in spite of my size—and my lack of experience at being an actual boy—I worked extra hard to prove myself at every task. I carried heavy, bulky logs that were used both for building new structures, and for keeping the fires going. I also helped the guards—includ-ing my mother—who kept watch at the camp's entry on the other side of the swamp, and I took messages back and forth to the hospital. I went a little fur-ther into the woods to gather wood, camouflage trails, and to watch for anyone who might be coming in our direction. I had become proficient at finding my way around the forest and back to camp without getting lost. I was observant, and good at remembering small details, such as the formations of the trees, the color of their bark. And although watching surgeries might not seem like some-thing a child—or even most adults—would like to do, I found it fascinating. My scientific mind prevented me from becoming squeamish during even the most gruesome surgeries.

I watched abdomens being cut open, exposing shiny intestines. When lungs had been damaged or diseased, I'd watch my father cut chest cavities open with a saw, in order to reach in and remove dead pieces of lungs—some with bullets still clinging to them. And I watched as feet and arms were amputated, sometimes without the benefit of anesthesia. To my father's credit, as well as the dedicated hospital workers, most of the surgery patients managed to survive. When they didn't survive, it was usually because of infections or diseases such as typhus or *gas gangrene*—a bacterial infection which causes body tissue to decay and die. In a real hospital these patients would have survived because the appropriate medications would have been easily accessible.

When you're little, your world is small, and you don't know any better, so whatever life you're living seems "normal." I didn't remember any actual "normal" life. We'd always been hungry and in desperate danger. I didn't remember not being dirty, not having lice, not having to be constantly on the alert. I didn't remember being free to be a child—to run and play and make noise, to have holidays, to have toys, and to just be silly. On the other hand, there were some activities that I did enjoy

I liked finding and bringing wood for the camp fire. I liked shinnying up trees to look for Germans. And one of my favorite activities was accompanying my mother on guard duty. Imagine the two of us holding off invaders! Mama wasn't more than five feet tall, and I was an under-sized seven year old. While she'd been trained in the basics of shooting a rifle, Mama was far from expert—and we both knew that a bigger, stronger man could easily take the gun away from her. But we were tough, and took our responsibilities seriously. The most important of which was making sure that anyone who tried to enter had the secret password.

One day, as we stood guard at the entry to the hospital island, several partisan leaders we didn't know approached us. Mama held up her gun as menacingly as she could, and demanded that they give her the password. They clearly were not happy about being given orders by a woman. Without being told, I slipped away to find Papa. Being extra careful not to fall off a moving log, I crossed the swamp, found Papa, and told him what was happening. He followed me back to the guard post, and let the men know they needed to obey the camp's rules— even when the orders were given by a woman. Once they understood that the little woman giving the orders was Mrs. Miasnik, they apologized, and praised her for being such an outstanding guard. Later, even though Papa and I teased her for being such a tough partisan, we were proud of her courage out there on her own with those big partisan men.

On March 10, 1943, the hospital staff put together a party to celebrate my eighth birthday. Since we had no flour and no oven, of course there was no birthday cake. Instead, they cooked my favorite potato soup. I didn't expect any gifts. And that was why I was particularly surprised when my parents said that they had something for me. I was confused because I couldn't imagine what this gift would be. Papa crouched down, put his hands lovingly on my shoulders, and looked me straight in the eyes, and spoke solemnly:

"Mirele, Mama and I are so proud of how you've conducted yourself during these terrible times. We know how hard it's been to be the only child in a partisan camp, and how frightening it is to always be in danger. You've never given us a moment of worry, and we depend on you. We are so lucky to have such a good and brave daughter. We wanted to give you a special gift for your birthday. We decided that you are now old enough, and responsible enough, to have a gun of your own."

And while I tried to make sense out of what Papa had just told me, Mama held out her hand to me. In it was a small, silver pistol with a pearl-handle—and it most definitely was not a toy. What a birthday surprise! I was thrilled, but wanted to look tough, so I managed to contain my smile. Carefully taking the gun from Mama, I felt its cold surface as I turned it over and around, admiring its pretty decorations. I knew better than to point it at anyone—including myself. Papa told me the gun had been taken from a German officer, who'd had it specially designed for his girlfriend.

With my best grown up voice, I thanked my parents, "*Mamele, Tatele,* thank you. This is the best gift I could ever receive. I promise to take good care of it." Eager to do some target practice, I was disappointed when my parents explained that I wouldn't be given bullets until I'd been trained to shoot. From that day forward, I proudly wore the gun in a side holster belted over my boyish military uniform. Now I felt like I was a real grown-up instead of the only child in the camp. And whenever I thought of it, I also tried to walk like a tough fighter. I was especially delighted when the other people in the camp made a big fuss over my gun and told me that I now was a real partisan!

I had always been skilled with my hands and anything mechanical, so I took great pride in dismantling, cleaning, oiling, and reassembling my own gun. Seeing my skill, and appreciating my attention to detail, the partisans soon trusted me to maintain their pistols and rifles. This intense process involved working carefully with a lot of small parts and screws—which was easy with my tiny fingers. I was all too aware that any mistakes I made would cause people to die.

Much as I loved having my own gun, and even though it made me feel safe and important, there came a day when it caused me a terrible crisis. I'd had to go to the bathroom, which is a nice way of saying that I had to find a tree to crouch behind and take care of my personal business. The holster was bulky on my little body, making it awkward to pull my pants down, so I took it off, and hung it on the nearest branch. When I was finished, I forgot to put the holster back on and left it where I'd hung it.

At first, I didn't realize I didn't have it, but when I finally noticed, I was overwhelmed by anxiety and fear. I ran back to the tree, but the holster was gone. Clearly, I wasn't as responsible as everyone thought, and they'd all soon know that I'd let them down—that I really was just a kid and not a partisan. The idea of disappointing my parents crushed my spirit. Since they would see that I wasn't wearing my holster—not to mention that I was crying hysterically, I had no choice but to tell them. I begged them to search the entire camp, which they did, but they couldn't find it. I was inconsolable.

After a few days, the Soviet commander of the camp walked slowly up to me, looking me straight in the eye. I was afraid of this huge, angry looking man whose bushy black mustache almost covered the entire bottom half of his face. He stood less than a foot away, looking straight down at me. My feet froze to the ground. Without saying a word, he reached into his coat's deep pocket and slowly brought out my holster and gun. He dangled it in front of me and finally spoke in a dark, gruff tone, "As you know, it is a crime for a partisan to lose a gun. I'll let you off this time, but do not let it happen again." Since I'd seen a partisan be shot for committing some crime, I just nodded at him. As he turned away, I saw him shake his head, and I thought I heard him laugh.

Spring was on the way and while we were glad that the punishing winter was finally leaving, for people living in the forest, summer had its own challenges. The worst of these was the scarcity of clean, drinkable water. Sometimes we were lucky and could save rain water. But most of the time, we had to take whatever we could find—usually swamp water from which we had to remove bugs, dirt, and other debris—and then boil it. While we appreciated the warm weather, along with the abundant wild berries and sweet tree sap, we did not appreciate the swarms of hungry, disease-carrying mosquitoes that thrived in the swamps. The biggest problem with summer, however, was a different kind of deadly swarm. Summer was the preferred time for the Germans to attack. And that's exactly what they did.

The partisans had put together a creative and complicated scouting system throughout the forest. Some scouts hid inside rotted-out tree trunks or entwined themselves amidst leafy branches. Others dug holes they could hide in, which they then camouflaged with ground-cover. Special sounds that mimicked animal noises were used as warning alerts whenever Germans were spotted. One of the most successful strategies for killing Germans was to wait until one left his group in order to go to relieve himself behind a tree. At his most vulnerable moment, a partisan would silently capture and drag him back to the camp. The prisoner would be interrogated about German actions in the forest. At the end of the interrogation, the prisoner would be killed.

The stealth, skill, and fierce reputation of the partisans created a sense of fear in the Germans, and they hated coming into the forest. No matter how careful the partisans were, however, they knew that at any moment the Germans might learn the location of our hospital. And eventually, that is exactly what happened. We got word that the Germans were coming in large numbers, and they planned to wipe us out. As if our daily existence wasn't already dangerous, we now had to figure out how to protect the patients. We couldn't stay there and fight, because we'd be trapped and killed. We couldn't leave the patients behind, but carrying them with us was impossible.

Despite our arguments, Papa made the decision that Mama and I should leave the hospital immediately, and return to the Jewish family camp. He told us he couldn't take care of evacuating the patients if he had to also worry about us. So reluctantly leaving him and all the others behind, Mama and I rushed to the family camp. When we arrived, we were relieved to know that the residents had prepared in advance for a surprise attack. They had built an emergency dugout nearby, beneath a massive rotted tree that had fallen to the ground. They camouflaged this hideout with dirt, leaves, and branches. Its only entrance was a small opening in the ground, in which—just to be on the safe side—they inserted a living tree, roots and all. With no time to spare, all twenty of us managed to squeeze into this shelter, with the last one in pulling the tree into place above him. We all held our breaths as we soon heard heavy footsteps plodding heavily toward us through the brush. As the footsteps came closer, we heard the harsh sounds of German voices over our pounding hearts. We expected to be discovered and shot within minutes.

But somehow, we got lucky. The clueless Germans tromped right over us without an inkling of what lay quivering in fear beneath them. As our breathing normalized, and our hearts calmed down, each of us silently thanked God for saving us once again from being slaughtered. Terrified that the Germans might come back, we stayed in the crowded shelter throughout the rest of the night. Finally, a scout let us know all was clear, and we quietly returned to our zemlyanka.

As the only child in the group, I was especially grateful to be alive, because I had heard about other groups in hiding where the children had been smothered so they wouldn't cry out in fear. Luckily for me, this group of adults didn't worry that I'd make noise. They understood that I hadn't been a child since the war began.

We were relieved a few days later, when a courier came to let us know that not only had Papa and the hospital staff all survived, but so had their carefully evacuated patients. Fortunately for all, the Germans had never found the hospital. Over the next few days, the patients and medical staff would return to the hospital in the forest.

Chapter 9
June 1944-March 1945: *Liberated but Not Free*

The relentless winter finally began to fade into a soft, sweet spring, and I had another birthday in the forest. Turning nine didn't really mean much to me, however, because time didn't really mean much to me. Although I had grown a bit taller, I hadn't moved up a grade in school, celebrated any holidays, or gone on summer vacations. Just as when I turned seven and eight, I didn't have a birthday party, and I certainly didn't get any new clothes or even any small surprise gifts. There was however, one huge surprise this spring—and it was bigger and better than anything I could have hoped for—if I had known how to hope.

This time, when we heard the familiar, yet still terrifying rumble of overhead planes, and waited breathlessly for explosions, we were stunned to see that instead of bombs, the planes were dropping men in parachutes! Soviet soldiers! Lots of them! We rushed out to the clearing where they were landing, to welcome them, and to our delight, they'd brought food, blankets and medicine. But the biggest surprises of all were the amazing notes they each carried.

These notes directed them all to find Dr. Miasnik in the partisans' Lipiczany Forest hospital. Papa was famous! As it turned out, one of these Soviet soldiers had been injured when he landed, and needed immediate surgery, so instead of him having to go out and find Papa, our group carried him straight to the hospital. On the way, he told us that everyone in the Soviet Army knew about the heroic accomplishments of Dr. Miasnik. Mama and I were so proud of him.

A few months later, we heard that the Soviet Army was on the way. Sure enough, in the early summer, the forest filled with the noise of approaching Soviet tanks crashing through the trees and underbrush. Even without today's electronic devices, news traveled fast, and partisans who had been hiding throughout the forest emerged to joyously greet our liberators. It looked as if we would soon be free to live normal lives. And even though I didn't really remember what a normal life was, I was just as ecstatic as everyone else! During those last weeks in the forest, whenever we saw Soviet soldiers we ran up to them with tears in our eyes, hugging and kissing them for being our saviors. I joined the adults in saluting the soldiers, and even kissed one's hand in gratitude. He hugged me and told my father he should be proud of such a courageous "son." Of course I was thrilled that he thought I was brave boy!

In the 18 months we'd been in the forest, our region of what had once been Poland went from being occupied by the Soviets (1939-1941), to being occupied by the Germans (1941-1944). Now, having been liberated by the Soviets, we were once again under their control, and although we didn't know it yet, we were now part of the Soviet Socialist Republic of Belarus.

Although I was overjoyed that the monstrous Germans were finally gone, I was nervous about what would happen next. I had been trained to always be on the alert for danger, but I'd had no training for being safe. I also knew that while we'd been "liberated," and would soon be living in an actual house, the rest of Europe was still fighting the Germans—and those Germans were determined to kill as many Jews as possible. So as far as I was concerned, there still was the chance that they'd come back for us. Adding to my anxiety was the fact that unlike the adults—who looked forward to returning to "normal" life—I had no memory of a normal life. I was anxious that I wouldn't be good at the challenges a normal life might bring, and that I'd disappoint my parents. Little did I know that the adults were just as nervous as I was. And with good reason.

One of the first benefits of liberation was the flood of news about what was going on in the world. We'd been so cut off from civilization in the forest, that it was a thrill to learn about the real world. Our excitement wore off, however, as we learned the Germans had executed millions of Jews in ghettos, concentration camps and death camps. Every day brought new reports of unspeakable horror—especially the news about the extermination of the Jews in the Lida ghetto in September of 1943. Over 4,000 Jews who had been trapped there were loaded onto cattle cars and shipped to Sobibor. Upon their arrival, they were murdered. Somehow, fourteen men had managed to escape the train and hide in the forest. They eventually found and joined the Bielski partisans.[8]

Ironically, while liberation brought us freedom from the Germans, we learned all too soon that there would be no real freedom under the Soviets. This was because the Soviet Communist government would control almost every aspect of our lives. First, they transported us from the forest in open trucks to Szczuczyn, a town in what is now Belarus. Then they assigned us to the houses in which we would live. They assigned jobs to the men—often without considering what jobs the men actually wanted, or for which they were qualified. Fortunately for us, the Soviets needed a doctor, so my father was appointed chief of staff of the local hospital. He was thrilled to be able to treat patients in a real building, where they had actual beds, as well as enough food and medicine. And while most of the men received very small salaries, we were also lucky that the Soviets paid Papa enough for us to live on without having to worry about our survival.

We were grateful that Papa came home to us every day, instead of having to spend so much time caring for injured partisans in the forest. Ironically, we still didn't see very much of him because he'd set up a small, makeshift doctor's office in an extra bedroom of our house, so at night and on weekends, he took care of his own patients. This allowed him to earn a little money on the side, which he carefully saved for an emergency. Papa knew all too well that there would always be an emergency.

The benefits of having a little extra money, however, did not make up for our general lack of freedom. The Soviets had a strict philosophy about private ownership of property: it wasn't allowed. Since the government controlled and distributed all property any way it saw fit, we couldn't own anything! The government also censored radio programs and movies, so we didn't know what was going on in the rest of the world. And since outgoing mail was also censored, the rest of the world had no idea what life was like under Soviet control. Our lack of freedom was not acceptable to my parents.

So while on the surface, it looked as if we had a good life, we were not happy that the Soviet government controlled our lives. Yes, we had a house to live in,

8 The Bielski partisan group was started by brothers who grew up in the village of Nowogródek, near Lida. They escaped from their ghetto and formed a fierce partisan group in the forest. The 2008 award-winning movie, "Defiance," which recounts their experiences, was based on Nechama Tec's 1993 book, *Defiance: The Bielski Partisans*.

enough food to eat, and I could go to school and explore the neighborhood. I didn't have to worry that I'd get killed or that my parents would be gone when I got home. Yes, it was wonderful that we weren't discriminated against for being Jewish, but living in a city where there were so few Jews was very strange and very sad. Whether we'd lived in Warsaw, Lida, or the forest, we'd always lived near or among Jewish people. We had always felt connected to a Jewish community. Now there was no Jewish community, so we kept to ourselves and didn't mingle with the townspeople. It might have been easier for me to adjust if I'd had some playmates, but there was no way I could trust the Christian children—or their parents—who, only a few weeks before, would have instantly turned me over to the Nazis. Living without freedom was not acceptable to my parents. They'd gone through too much to settle for being under Soviet control.

In my loneliness, I became more and more quiet and withdrawn. This changed unexpectedly when I met a sweet Jewish girl my age named Halinka. She and her refugee parents had just arrived in Szczuczyn. They were grateful to find another Jewish family. And just like me, Halinka was hoping to find a friend. We bonded instantly and poured our hearts out to each other. I was surprised to learn that Halinka and her family had come to the Lida ghetto shortly after we'd escaped. Within a few days, they were rounded up to be deported. Halinka was only seven when she, her parents, and the rest of the Jews had to line up and began boarding the train to a death camp. As they waited their turn, Halinka's parents suddenly slipped a small scrap of paper into her hand. On it was written the address of a friendly Gentile woman they knew in town. They told Halinka to sneak out of line, go straight to the water fountain, and from there, fade into the crowd, and then go find the Gentile's house. Fortunately, Halinka didn't look Jewish, so she was able to mingle with the townspeople, and escape the deportation line.

She found her way to the address, and again, was lucky. The family immediately took her in, cared for her as if she were their own daughter. And they raised her as a Catholic. Meanwhile, her parents had managed to jump off the moving train and escape to the forest. They eventually were able to find and join the Bielski partisans. After liberation, Halinka's parents returned to Lida, hoping desperately that their little girl had survived. They were overjoyed when they found the Catholic family that had taken her in. But they all were in for a sad surprise. Halinka had grown to love her foster family—and they loved her. So when her strange-looking refugee parents came for her, she felt torn from both sides. Reluctantly, she left the comfortable place that had become her home, and the people who had become her family, to join her parents on a very uncomfortable journey.

They eventually managed to connect with the Soviets, and that's how they ended up in Szczuczyn. As I listened to Halinka, I thought about how her safe, warm, well-fed days with the Catholic family contrasted with my dangerous, cold, and hungry life in the partisans. In a way, it seemed as if her life had been easier than mine. But I was sad for her because she'd been separated from her parents and had suffered greatly: first when she thought they had died, and second, when they suddenly reappeared and reclaimed her. It reminded me of my own experience with the kind and courageous Catholic "Auntie" who took me in to live with her and her daughter on their farm outside Lida. I wondered what would have happened to me if I had been forced to live there permanently. That thought gave me a weird feeling in my stomach, so I let go of it as soon as it entered my mind.

The Soviets reopened the schools, but in the absence of real teachers, they just assigned various educated people to instruct us. The result was that a bookkeeper might end up teaching English, and a lawyer might end up teaching math. Because of my age, Mama enrolled me in third grade even though I'd never been to school! Fortunately, she'd taught me to read and write in Polish so I wasn't totally illiterate. I was nervous at first, but I was a quick learner. It helped that the other kids were also uneducated, so I didn't feel ignorant in comparison! We were quite a motley group—most of us had been on the run, living outdoors, or in hiding for a big part of our short lives. We must have been a real challenge to our teachers since none of us were used to being quiet, or sitting up straight in desks in neat rows, or raising our hands if we had a question or comment.

We didn't have experience interacting with polite society—or following rules that seemed childish to us. Why on earth would anyone have to ask permission to go to the bathroom? And we weren't used to being treated as if we were mindless little kids, so we could get irritated if we felt disrespected. Despite our young ages, none of us felt like children. We all were old beyond our years. We were used to dealing with starvation and murderous Germans—not verbs or fractions! Some of us were used to handling weapons. And one of us carried a pink pearl-handled gun in a holster slung around her hips!

One day after school, I walked through the streets, just exploring the town, much like I would have explored my surroundings in the forest. Suddenly, a tall Soviet soldier loomed over me. Apparently the sight of a nine-year old strolling through the streets with a holstered gun caught his attention. He reached down and snatched it away from me. Indignant at his rude behavior, I stiffened, looked up defiantly, and proclaimed loudly in Russian, that I was a partisan, and he should give me my gun back immediately. This struck him as humorous, and he laughed at me. Now highly insulted, I ran home crying—something I never would have done in the forest! Mama hugged me and explained that many Soviet soldiers were still fighting the Germans in western Europe, and they needed all the weapons they could get. She added that the soldier would be sending my gun to them in order to kill Germans. That sounded like a good idea, and since I didn't need it anymore—or have any choice—I was happy that at least it would be put to good use.

Living in a house, sleeping in a bed, eating regular meals, being clean, attending school, and going "gun-less" would not be the only changes in my lifestyle. Since I no longer had to look like a boy, it was no longer necessary for my head to be shaved. It was interesting to see hair growing on my head, and I was fascinated by the difference it made in my appearance. I was beginning to look like an actual girl. And despite my protests, I even wore dresses! Tough, competent, fierce partisan Miriam was being replaced by an unprotected, awkward, young girl. And I didn't like it.

During wartime, some women had been brutally victimized. Others had been fearless nurses or fierce fighters. Now, after the war was over, girls were subject to a lot of social restrictions. We were supposed to be quiet and polite, learn to cook and do needlework, wear nice outfits, and above all, act like young ladies. Boys, on the other hand, could still dress in comfortable, mis-matched boy-clothes, and have adventures, fun, and freedom. I had liked being a boy! Unfortunately for me, my parents were eager to have their daughter back—and they didn't seem to mind that their "son" was gone! Losing my partisan-self wasn't my only challenge. Adults viewed and treated me like a child—something I didn't remember ever being.

Another big worry for me was that in over two years, we'd had no news about what had happened to our relatives in Warsaw. And despite the devastating stories we'd heard about the total destruction of the Warsaw ghetto, I desperately held on to the hope that one day I'd see my grandparents, Aunt Ala, and Uncle Tadek again.

Amidst my anxieties, and challenges, I was sometimes surprised by an occasional moment of pure joy. On Sunday afternoons, Szczuczyn residents often spent their leisure time visiting with friends in the town square. And that's just what Mama, Papa, and I were doing one lovely August Sunday afternoon, when a bedraggled group of Soviet soldiers passed by on their way west to fight the Germans. When a particularly gaunt and sad looking soldier spotted us, a strange expression spread across his face. He slipped away from his comrades and as if he knew us, walked straight up to Papa. Somehow, among all the people in the town square, he had recognized that Papa was Jewish.

They instantly engaged in an intense conversation in Yiddish. Mama and I soon joined in, and as was so common among Jewish Holocaust survivors, we eagerly exchanged life-stories. We always hoped someone would have information about a missing loved one. As we chattered on about our families, friends, and wartime experiences, he continued to gaze at me. Then, as if we were relatives, he reached out to me, patted my head, and stroked my hair.

He asked Mama and Papa if I was their child. My parents nodded, and the soldier swept me up into his arms, held me close, and began to sob. It felt weird and I didn't know what to do, but since my parents didn't seem concerned, I didn't try to get away. When he regained his composure, he put me down, and explained, "This is the first living Jewish child I have seen in so very long. I didn't think that any had survived. Thank you for saving a precious Jewish child."

On Sundays, when bad weather kept us from relaxing in the square, we enjoyed going to the local movie theater. Of course there were no Hollywood movies—no musicals, no mushy love stories, silly Mickey Mouse cartoons, or Laurel and Hardy comedies. All they ever showed were violent Soviet war movies, which were filled with hideous images of unspeakable German brutality. You'd probably think that German brutality would be the last thing we'd want to see, but in this case, we actually got a thrill from it. This was because no matter how awful the Germans were in these movies—and they were awful—they always lost in the end. Badly. And after they lost, they were all brutally killed. And each time a German died, we all hollered our approval, applauded wildly, and stamped our feet. It was great!

One day, something happened that at first seemed wonderful, but turned out to be very dangerous. Out of the blue, Papa was ordered to report to the office of the Szczuczyn's Communist leader. This order made us nervous, because the government could decide that Papa would have to go work in a different town. They could even decide he should dig ditches instead of performing surgery. Papa's anxiety increased when the leader told him that a special message for him had arrived from Moscow. Papa was relieved to learn that he had been awarded the prestigious *Orden Lenina*.[9] He needed to go all the way to Moscow to attend a formal award ceremony where he would be honored.

While Mama and I were proud that Papa was being recognized by the government, he did not share our happiness. And after much soul-searching, he decided not to go to Moscow to collect his award. He understood that this honor could not possibly make up for the lack of freedom in our lives. He looked at it as a bribe. After suffering for so long under the Germans, he did not

9 The prestigious *Orden Lenina* (Order of Lenin) was the highest civilian award given by the Soviet government.

want us to live the rest of our lives under harsh Soviet control. Papa and Mama knew that the Soviets would never let us leave the country. They also knew that any attempts to do so would be punishable by imprisonment, exile in mercilessly cold and barren Siberia or even death. As former partisans, whose quick wits, skills, and determination had allowed them to survive the Nazis, my parents decided that despite the risks, we had to get out of the Soviet Union as soon as possible. So they carefully devised a plan, and planned to act upon it quickly. Unfortunately, just when they were ready to put it into action, Mama and I became sick with whooping cough.[10]

The constant prolonged stress, plus the physical challenges of malnutrition and exhaustion, along with the harsh living conditions in the forest, had taken a toll on my young body. And since I hadn't been near children, I hadn't been exposed to, or built up any immunity to the usual childhood diseases. It seemed as if every germ in the air was using me for a target. My coughing was so violent that my handkerchiefs were always soaked with blood. I was confined to bed for several months, and despite Papa's care, and Mama's constant vigilance, I kept getting weaker and sicker. It seemed as if my bed had become my prison, and I wouldn't be getting out alive.

Adding to my misery was the fact that since I had to stay isolated from everyone, I couldn't go to school. So while my classmates made steady progress, I fell even further behind. Making my days even worse was that Halinka was not allowed to visit. It took over a year for me to even partially recover my health, and it seemed as if I'd never be completely healthy again.

All during that year of endless health problems, we never lost our hopes of gaining our freedom. In fact, since my parents each had brothers in America who would help us, getting to the United States became our goal. We talked often about reuniting with our relatives in the "land of milk and honey." And while I wasn't sure what that meant, I wondered what it would be like to live in a country that hadn't been destroyed by war. So one way or another, we had to get to the US. All we had to do was 1: stay healthy; 2: accumulate some money; 3: figure out how to escape the Soviets; and 4: Cross the Atlantic Ocean!

My mother, Bronka Miasnik, was an amazing woman. She seemed quiet and ladylike, but she had a strength that made arguments melt in their tracks. The determination she exhibited during our 18 months in the Lida ghetto, and the following 18 months in the forest, didn't stop with liberation. When Mama was confronted with a problem, she didn't waste time and emotional energy on it. And she didn't feel sorry for herself. She became focused, analyzed the problem,

10 Whooping cough is a highly contagious disease that causes victims to cough violently. These coughs have a high-pitched whooping sound.

and brainstormed possible solutions in her head. Eventually, she would come up with a plan. Once she had a plan, nothing and no one could stop her.

So as soon as Mama had recovered her health, and I had finally grown a bit stronger, the next thing we needed in order to get out of the Soviet Union was some money. Naturally, Mama decided she would just go out and get some. Better yet, since each country only recognized its own money, she would go out and get some gold. Well, the only place she knew of where there would be some gold, was the very place where she'd buried it: in the barn behind our house in the Lida ghetto. So that's where she decided to go.

Since there was no one to take care of me while Papa was working—which was most of the time—Mama decided that she and I would return to the Lida ghetto together. Of course Papa tried to stop her. He used every logical argument that he could think of. And of course he knew the whole time that his arguments would have no effect. He sadly waved goodbye to us at the train station. Just as we had wondered if we'd ever see him again every time he'd said goodbye to us in the forest, he probably wondered if he'd ever see us again.

We arrived in Lida a few hours later, and as we walked toward the former ghetto, we looked around the pretty little town we once had loved, and shuddered at the damage it had suffered. When we got to the former ghetto, we immediately saw that the barbed-wire fences that had caged so many Jews were gone. Just like the Jews. Gone. Strangely, some of the homes in the ghetto had remained intact, and were now inhabited by their original owners. When we turned a corner and saw the house where we and so many other terrified Jews had lived, my stomach quivered, and I felt nauseous. I wondered what had happened to them. I especially wondered about little Tuska.

My thoughts were interrupted by the crazed barking of an angry dog. I began to sweat and looked up at Mama to see what she would do. I was frightened because I knew she wouldn't back down from danger. I breathed a long sigh of relief when she turned away from the house and we started walking in the opposite direction. I was glad that she'd decided that the best course of action would be to get some help. And she knew just where to get it.

Unbeknownst to me, some of our partisan friends had returned to Lida. Somehow Mama had been able to track them down, and they were overjoyed to see us. Mama explained what we were trying to do, told them about the dog, and asked for their help. They were only too eager to protect her during our mission. Proud to be fighters again, they put on ammunition belts and carried their rifles conspicuously as they escorted us back to the ghetto house. It was as if they had one last partisan mission to accomplish. The home's current occupants, a middle-aged couple, angrily stormed out of the front door to confront us, but stopped in their tracks when they saw the angry, armed, and determined group.

Following the partisans' orders, the homeowners bitterly raised their arms in the air, and then watched in fury as Mama and I calmly walked to the barn in the back yard. We immediately noticed that the yard had been dug up in several places—the homeowner had been searching for buried Jewish treasure. Too bad he hadn't thought to look under the step just inside the barn's door. We could see the man squirming as we moved the step and dug up our precious treasure.

Excited by our victory, and eager to see Papa's face when we returned with our gold, we rushed back to the train station. Once we were settled in our seats, Mama asked the conductor about the train's schedule, only to be rudely told it would not be stopping in Szczuczyn. Unruffled by what seemed like terrible news to me, Mama merely held up a half-full bottle of vodka, smiled sweetly, and told the conductor that he could have it if he could arrange to stop for just a minute in Szczuczyn. His mood immediately changed and he assured Mama that the train would stop wherever she wanted it to! Good thing Mama knew the power of vodka!

Upon our victorious return, Papa was thrilled with our achievement, and proud of Mama's clever tactics. Now that we were reasonably healthy, and thanks to Mama, had acquired some money, our little family was ready to proceed to the third step of our escape: figuring out how to escape from the giant prison that was the Soviet Union.

Soon, yet another one of Papa's grateful former patients would come to our rescue.

Chapter 10
March 1945: *Lublin and First Love*

When we'd first arrived in Szczuczyn, Papa had saved a deathly ill Soviet Air Force colonel by performing a difficult emergency operation. Upon fully recovering his health, the colonel couldn't thank Papa enough, and promised he would always help him if ever the need should arise. Coincidentally, just as my parents were trying to figure out how to get out of the Soviet Union, the colonel's brigade was ordered to go to central Poland, and the colonel came to say goodbye to Papa. During their farewells, Papa realized that the only way for us to escape the restrictions of the Soviets was to return to the place where millions of Jews had been exterminated: Poland. Papa asked the colonel to take us with him on the military train—and despite the risks involved, the colonel readily agreed.

As with our previous escapes, Mama and Papa kept their plans secret from me until almost the last minute. They took this precaution so that I wouldn't accidentally let others know about our plans. When Mama told me that we were leaving Szczuczyn *the next day*, and going to Poland, of all places, I was stunned. We all knew that Poland was a place of death for Jews. And by now I was old enough to question my parents' decisions. Despite my repeated questions, however, my parents avoided giving me an answer that made sense to me. All they said was that we had to get out immediately—going wherever we could while we still had a chance. And we had the chance to go to Poland, so we were going.

Careful to avoid the notice of our neighbors, we rushed around packing the few things we could carry. My parents had already hidden their gold coins inside the lining of a small wooden box. Unlike money, it could be used in any country. While Mama and I packed, Papa stayed busy seeing patients in our little home office. He still had a few people in the waiting area when we heard a rumble outside. Papa knew this was the military truck that the colonel had arranged to pick us up. Without any explanation, Papa excused himself from his patients, picked up his suitcase that had been placed by our front door, and joined Mama and me as we silently slipped out of the house together.

We climbed into the bed of the truck, and laid down flat so we wouldn't be seen. The truck headed for the train station. We snuggled together and tried to reassure each other that all would be well. We knew, however, that as soon as Papa's patients got tired of waiting for him to come back, they would look for him. Once they'd discovered that he was gone—that all three of us were gone—these patients, who had depended on my father for their health needs, would immediately report us to the authorities. And of course, that's just what they did. I still wonder how people who had been so grateful to my father for his kind and expert care, would so easily endanger him and his family.

The truck driver took us right to the station where we scrambled out of truck and proceeded to find the train. There had been so much weirdness for so many years that people had grown used to strange sights. A family emerging from the back of a truck and rushing to find a train was not considered unusual. The colonel had told Papa which train to board. so he easily found it. As we climbed the steps, we saw that the Soviet secret police were already conducting a man-hunt—or in our case, a "family-hunt." We shuddered with the knowledge that we were the targets of their search.

Naturally, the police had begun their search in what they'd thought was the most likely place: the train station. Much to the frustration and inconvenience of the many passengers, the police carefully searched every car on every departing *civilian* train. Of course it never occurred to them to search *military* trains. If it hadn't been so terrifying, it would have been funny. All these tough police-men ordering everyone off and on the wrong trains created chaos and anger in the crowded station.

Good thing we hadn't been aware that our situation was even worse than we thought. We soon learned that Papa had been identified as a highly wanted criminal. The authorities had officially accused him of robbing the municipal hospital—and an award had been offered for his capture. Funny how when he actually had arranged for hospitals to be robbed in order to provide for the par-tisans, he never got caught. Now, the only thing he'd done that was illegal was to try to leave the USSR, and he'd become a wanted man. Had any of us been spotted and captured, we would have been sent to a prison camp in Siberia.

We found our seats, and held our breaths until the train chugged out of the station. Then we settled in and began to worry about what life might bring us next. The last thing I'd expected was for there to be a party on the train. But that's pretty much what happened. The soldiers, who'd heard of Papa, welcomed us with warmth and respect. They stayed up late telling stories of their battles. And when Papa began singing patriotic songs in his beautiful voice, the soldiers joined right in. Along with joyfully singing patriotic songs together, we all shared our food. During the slow, uneventful two-day trip, I was probably only one who got any sleep. When we arrived in Bialystok, Poland, we said goodbye to the soldiers and wished them well. We then boarded a civilian train that would take us to Lublin.

Upon our arrival in Lublin, we were grateful to have a place to live available to us. We would be sharing an apartment with friends from the partisans. Sadly, after just a few days, it became clear that we weren't welcome to stay any longer. We were fortunate that Papa was able to find another place for us, in what had once been a store. It was located inside a courtyard, and we would be sharing one large open room with several other families. There was a kitchen area at one end as well as a bathroom that everyone would have to share. Even though it was often in use when I needed it, I was glad that the bathroom was indoors! Since we were the first to move in, we had the place to ourselves for a few wonderful days—and we were grateful for the peace and quiet.

Ironically, our first night in this new residence was also the first night of *Passover*: March 29, 1945.[11] Just like the Jews who had escaped from enslavement in Egypt, we had escaped the Germans, and then the Soviets. And while our journey would not take 40 years, sometimes it felt as if it were taking even longer. The last time my family had celebrated Passover was in 1939, when I'd been only four years old. I had no memory of it, but I deeply felt my parents' loneliness, and anger at the absence of our relatives on this, our first holiday in six years.

That night, Mama and Papa told me about Passover, and the Jews' 40-year journey out of slavery in Egypt. They explained the "Four Questions" of a traditional Passover dinner known as a *Seder*. The first, "How is this night different from all other nights?" had particular significance for us. As we sat on our hard chairs, just the three of us, with no food to eat, or traditional wine to drink, my parents sorrowfully reminisced about Seders of their past. When we could stay

11   As recounted in the Old Testament's Exodus, *Passover (Pesach)* is a Jewish holiday celebrating the Jews' escape or "exodus," from Egypt.

awake no longer, we pushed our chairs together and laid down across them. Our first night in Lublin was definitely different from all other nights.

The next morning, Papa was up at daybreak, and since we were terribly hungry, he decided to go out and try to buy some food. Unfortunately, a group of young antisemitic boys had been hanging out by our gate, and decided to use him for target practice. They hurled rocks at him, screaming that he was a dirty Jew and had no business there. They demanded to know why he hadn't been killed. Luckily, a market was nearby and Papa was able to slip inside before getting seriously injured. His good luck, however, was only temporary. His attackers who had waited for him to come out of the store, resumed throwing rocks at him. They followed him all the way home, screaming, "We know what to do with dirty Jews: Kill them!" Fortunately, they stopped at the gate to our courtyard. Shocked by what had happened, we decided that Mama, who did not look Jewish, would do the shopping from then on.

The following day, feeling indignant about the attack on Papa, and curious about what dangers might be lurking beyond our gate, I cautiously stepped outside. I'd only ventured a few steps when—as if they'd been waiting for another victim—a gang of boys swarmed around me, pelting me with rocks and screaming, "Here's another dirty Jew!" I screamed and ran back through our courtyard and into the house. I didn't tell anyone what had happened, because I didn't want to worry anyone. I also didn't want to get in trouble for going outside the courtyard alone. Needless to say, I never went outside the courtyard again unless an adult was with me.

Our few precious days of privacy soon ended as the other residents began to arrive. Eventually, there were 18 people and lots of beds in that one open room. Since it was crowded there was no sense of personal space. The living conditions were stressful, but, as always, we were careful to be respectful of each other. I wasn't bothered by the situation because I'd lived in far worse. I also wasn't bothered because among these new housemates, there was one who was particularly interesting to me.

He was a handsome 15-year old boy, who was the only survivor of his whole family. Although I've forgotten his name, I clearly remember that he was tall and strong, had beautiful hazel eyes, and a mop of uncontrollable brown hair. I looked up to him because he was brave, and reminded me of the partisans. I was impressed that he didn't mind going out on the streets where he knew the Poles would attack him. In fact, I think he might have enjoyed these confrontations because he always inflicted much more damage than he received. I trusted him. And even though he wasn't quite an adult, I felt safe when he took me out on the streets. He always made sure to shield me from any attackers. This was all new for me. Being protected by a brave, handsome young man who lived in my apartment, and who enjoyed spending time with me, was a source of many exciting and conflicting emotions!

Adding to my emotional confusion was my sudden delight in being a girl! For the first time since we'd left the partisans, I didn't miss being able to act like a boy. I even wanted to be pretty. And although I didn't know the word yet, I definitely had a "crush" on him. We spent more and more time together, and during that time, my heart often fluttered, my mouth would go dry, and my stomach would clench and unclench with anxiety. I became awkward and bashful around him, always worrying that I'd say or do something silly that would cause him to avoid me. At the same time, I looked forward to the moments when he saw me—his eyes would light up as he smiled at me. Other than with my family, I'd never been the person that caused someone's eyes to light up. And I liked it.

One afternoon when he and I had gone out for a walk, something different happened. He took my hand, looked into my eyes, and told me that he was so glad he had me to talk to. Then, when I didn't blink or take my hand away, he asked me if I felt the same way about him. I didn't know what was more astonishing—that he was holding my hand, looking into my eyes, or that he told me that I was important to him! None of these things had ever happened to me before. Combined with my newly emerging hormones, this information caused my heart to flutter and my brain to spin! Fortunately, my years of having to hide my emotions proved to be helpful at that moment, allowing me to appear calm. And then I told him I felt the same way about him. We both exhaled and laughed with relief.

And then our pent-up words flooded out. My eyes teared up when he spoke about losing his parents, his home, and everything he had ever known. His eyes showed sympathy as I told him about my hard time with the partisans. He was surprised when I told him how my head had been shaved, and I dressed like a boy. He smiled when I told him how independent and powerful I'd felt as a boy, and how hard it had been to go back to being a girl. He laughed when I said that because of him, I was finally glad to be a girl again. He took my hand, looked softly in my eyes, and told me that he was glad, too.

Hiding our feelings for each other was not easy in our crowded apartment. There was no privacy. I'm sure the adults noticed this new development, and were keeping a careful eye on us, but they never mentioned it. I didn't mention it either, because I was afraid my father would force us to stay away from each other. We looked forward to the moments when we could slip away to a little corner in the courtyard, or take a walk. Relieved and grateful that we could speak honestly with each other, we shared our hopes and dreams for the future. No matter how much time we spent together, we never ran out of things to talk about—especially when it came to our war experiences. And with the certainty of young love, we even promised to get together after the war. Our moments of normalcy together reminded me of those connect-the-dots pictures where you have to draw in the lines in order to see the whole image. Each moment with this boy was like being in a little dot of normalcy. When we were together, I felt as if our picture was complete. I felt alive with joy and optimism. The time spent between the dots seemed empty and pointless.

Despite the challenges of living in such crowded circumstances, as well as the lack of money and the constant presence of angry Poles, our lives took on a sense of routine. Because we were relatively safe and had enough to eat, we were able to keep painful memories from affecting our day to day existence. That changed when we started hearing about the atrocities of the German's nearly successful campaign to murder all the Jews of Europe. In Poland alone, over three million Jews had been killed. And to our mind-numbing shock, this number included the more than 400,000 Jews who had been deported from the Warsaw ghetto.

This news was more than my mother could bear. Never one to sit around doing nothing when something needed to be done, she decided to go to Warsaw to find out what had happened to the city—and to our family. Of course, Papa pleaded with her not to go. It was still so dangerous, and what she would find would be so upsetting, and how would she manage on her own? Papa rarely failed at anything, but when it came to talking Mama out of doing something she was determined to do, he didn't stand a chance. Unrealistic as it might have been, Mama still believed that she would find her parents, her sister, Ala, and our other relatives. Stranger things had happened in the survivor community, and so we all held on to the hope that a miracle would happen for us.

Mama wasn't afraid to go to Warsaw on her own because she didn't look Jewish, and she was fluent in Warsaw's dialect of Polish. She wouldn't attract the attention of antisemites. Plus she knew the city well, and was confident that she wouldn't get lost and need someone's help. When she said goodbye to us, we could see a glow in her eyes that mirrored the determination in her heart. Unfortunately, when she arrived in Warsaw, her shock at what she saw was almost overwhelming. This once world-famous, beautiful and thriving city, where Jews had lived for almost 800 years, was in total ruins. The streets where we had lived had vanished. It was as if they had never been filled with homes, shops, and noisy crowds of people living busy lives. Despite having been born in Warsaw, and having lived there all her life, Mama didn't see a familiar face as she walked the streets. She felt like she was visiting another planet. A horribly damaged and hopeless planet.

Drawing on her fierce determination to overcome her fears, Mama made her way to what had been the Warsaw ghetto. What she saw was beyond her belief. For as far as she could see, there was nothing but a vast, rubble-filled field. Almost as if she were watching a movie, Mama envisioned the field filled with thousands of doomed Jews bravely going about their daily lives, in spite of the unimaginable horror that was coming their way. She finally understood what had happened to our family, and sank to the ground, sobbing uncontrollably. Clearly, there was no reason to stay in Warsaw. Haunted by ghosts, Mama turned and slowly walked back to the train station, where she waited for the train that would take her back to Lublin. Her hopes defeated by all she had seen and felt in Warsaw, she was relieved when the train arrived and she found a seat.

Unlike the somber atmosphere in the train on the way to Warsaw, the passengers going to Lublin were lively and seemed to be full of plans. Mama was lost in her own thoughts until the woman next to her struck up a conversation. Assuming that my mother was a Gentile, the woman gushed about her beautiful—formerly Jewish—home and her plans to make sure no Jews ever reclaimed it. Now alert to the conversations around her, Mama was stunned to realize that the lively passengers were hate-filled antisemites. The general theme of their loud conversations was that they were glad so many Jews had been exterminated. Their biggest fear was that a few surviving Jews might straggle back and reclaim their homes and possessions. The Poles were determined to make sure this didn't happen. In order to avoid talking with any of these people, Mama pretended to sleep for the rest of the trip.

Papa and I welcomed Mama home with relief and joy. Later that night, as she recounted her experiences to him, they decided that Poland was not a safe place for Jews. As usual, the decision to leave came quickly. Unfortunately, it would take longer to figure out exactly *how* to leave. Fortunately, Papa's resourcefulness—along with a handy bottle of vodka—came to our rescue. Somehow, he'd found a Soviet soldier who was driving a truck to Czechoslovakia. In exchange for the vodka, the soldier agreed to take us with him. Czechoslovakia seemed like as good a place as any, just as long as it wasn't filled with antisemitic Poles! Again, as usual, I was not told that we were leaving until the last minute—and again, I was not allowed to say goodbye to anyone, not even that very special boy.

Chapter 11
April-May 1945: *Leaving Poland—Again!*

We left that evening, and were fortunate that in spite of his being drunk, the Soviet soldier was able to deliver us safely to a small city in Czechoslovakia the next morning. We wandered around until we found a group of Polish Jewish refugees who had also decided to get out of Poland. We joined them, feeling relieved to be able to talk with people who shared and understood our experiences. We learned that they were among the many Jews being assisted by various Jewish "relief agencies."[12] These agencies provided a variety of services to survivors who were fleeing both antisemitism and the Soviets.

Thinking that Hungary would be safe since it had been liberated by the Soviets, the relief agency had arranged a place for the group to stay in Budapest. Since we'd previously lived under harsh Soviet rule in Szczuczyn, we knew Budapest actually would not be a good place for us. Since we were desperate to leave Poland, however, and had no other options, Mama and Papa decided we should join the group.

Two days later when we arrived in Budapest, our group was directed to our next "home." My eyes lit up when I saw the beautiful large apartment building.

---

12   Relief Agencies: Organizations that help Jews who are in need. The largest and most well know of these is the American Jewish Joint Distribution Committee (Known as the "JOINT"), which was founded in 1914, and provided money to help Jews escape the Nazis during the war, and then find safe housing after the war.

My excitement at possibly living in comfort was dashed when I went inside and saw how crowded it was. So many other homeless Jews had been packed into the apartment building, that there wasn't enough room for us to settle in. Most of the furniture had been removed, and people filled every corner of every room, and even overflowed into hallways. We ended up sleeping wherever we could find a place on the floor.

There also weren't enough bathrooms, and the toilets and sinks were disgusting. Life outside the building was also miserable. The Soviets had liberated Budapest from the Germans in April 1945, but as we'd already experienced, living conditions under the Soviets were harsh. There never seemed to be enough of even the basics needed for daily life. The Soviets were particularly restrictive on food supplies, so once again, we were often hungry. Amongst our many problems, one of the worst was our inability to understand the Hungarian language. And, of course, the Hungarians could not understand us—not that they wanted to.

Then, as sometimes happens, everything changed. Well, almost everything. We'd been in Budapest a couple of weeks when in the midst of all our misery, something extraordinary happened. On May 7, 1945, the war ended. Crowds, delirious with joy, celebrated the defeat of the Germans, and welcomed Hungarian soldiers home. There were parades almost every day. It was a huge non-stop party for everyone—everyone, that is, except the Jews. While we were of course joyful that the war was finally over, and that the despicable Germans had finally been beaten, our joy was overshadowed by the reality that millions of Jews had been brutalized and murdered. The ones who had survived no longer had homes to return to. Every new day brought more stories of the monstrous crimes the Nazis had committed against the Jews. And with every story, my heart broke a little more as I pictured my beloved Aunt Ala, my precious grandmothers, and other dear relatives who'd probably suffered similar fates. So yes, the war had ended, but it was too late for the Jews.

After so many years of keeping my emotions buried deeply inside, it now seemed as if anything would start me sobbing with heart-wrenching sadness. Especially a song. One afternoon, a Polish Jewish woman inside the apartment building began singing a beautiful old Yiddish song, "I Wish to See My Home Again." Every Polish Jewish survivor within earshot had the same wish. And no matter what anyone was doing at that particular moment, we all started crying as if we were part of one huge broken heart. And even though I wasn't sure what having a real home meant, agony at not having one, coursed through my body. I rushed outside so no one would see me crying like a little kid.

On my way to a quiet corner in the courtyard, I saw a feeble and raggedy old Jew who still wore his filthy, tattered, concentration camp striped uniform. He seemed to be in his own world, staring off into the distance. Just looking at him made me quiver with emotions, and I inched closer to him. I hoped my presence wouldn't anger or make him sad. I waited briefly for him to notice me, and then spoke softly to him in Yiddish, asking where he had been during the war.

At first he seemed surprised by my question, but after a moment, his eyes met mine, and he asked me my name. I told him, "Mirele." At that moment, an unbreakable connection between us was made. Even after all these years, I clearly remember our conversation.

"Mirele, Mirele," he repeated. "Such a lovely name. Mirele, where are your parents?"

They are here with me." I responded. "We survived in the partisans."

Again, he seemed surprised. How could a little girl have been in the partisans? After a short pause, he told me that he'd been in Treblinka. And he told me about this camp, where Jews were sent to their deaths. He told me about losing his family, about the gruesome deaths from cold, overwork, and starvation. This information was stunning to me. Suddenly my mind was filled with images of my grandparents' terrible deaths in *Treblinka*.

"Mirele," he asked, "have you ever heard the song, 'Treblinka?'" I shook my head, and then he sang it to me. Even though every phrase burned through my brain and sliced through my heart, I couldn't run away—I was frozen to the spot.

Treblinka

In a small town fairly early in the morning
there is worry, noise and chaos
people half-naked the fear is great
"Jews!" they yell, "Out of your houses!"

Gendarmes, police, Ukrainians—
to kill the Jews is their aim
they hit and they shoot
there is panic and fear
they force the Jews to the trains

A pen cannot describe
how the wheels are turning
the wagons are full

they are sending millions of Jews
to their deaths in Treblinka
And our brothers
on the other side of the sea
they cannot feel our bitter taste
they cannot feel our bitter fear
that every hour we await our death

The war will someday come to an end
and the world will shudder in fear
the Jewish heart is filled with pain
nobody can feel our pain

Rivers of tears will flow
when one day will be found
the largest graveyard in the world
there are laying millions of Jews
of kiddush hashem*
in Treblinka,
in Treblinka

—Composer Unknown

**"of kiddush hashem"* means to become sacred in God's eyes.

The combination of Soviet controlled living conditions, antisemites and poverty, made it was clear that there was no future for us in Budapest. So just like thousands of other Jewish nomads, we packed up our few belongings, and continued on with what seemed to be an endless journey. Constantly traveling from place to place, we were always just a few steps ahead of the Soviets. It was like outrunning hot lava from a volcano. This time we were headed to Romania because that's where the group leader who was helping us said we had to go. Once aboard yet another train, and seated comfortably, we embarked on the first leg of the trip. It seemed as normal as possible under the circumstances. All too soon, however, it would become treacherous.

The next day, we got off the train in a small town near the Carpathian Mountains which separated Hungary and Romania. We joined a group of 15 other Jewish refugees, ranging in age from pre-teen to middle-aged. I was shocked to learn that we would have to trek over the mountains and then sneak in to Romania. But we didn't have time to feel sorry for ourselves. As soon as the adults had received their instructions from our guide, we wasted no time in embarking on this leg of our journey.

We started walking. And we continued walking. We walked most of the day, until we reached a forest. Having lived in a forest for 18 months, we felt at home in this wilderness. The others, however, were not so comfortable. We walked through the forest until we arrived at the foot of the Carpathian Mountains, and began to climb. None of us carried very much, but carrying anything at all uphill became impossible, and some of the people began to just drop their belongings, and leave them behind. It had grown cold and we were all hungry. This was particularly hard on me because the strenuous physical activity weakened my body, and I had serious trouble breathing. Then I started coughing, and several times I panicked because it felt as though I would suffocate.

Somehow, we made it across the mountain. Then we broke up into small groups so we could cross the border without being noticed. Once in Romania, we found a train station and boarded a train for our destination: a small city in the mountains named Turda, whose small Jewish population welcomed Jewish refugees. Upon our arrival, we were directed to a compound consisting of several small cottages on the edge of town. This compound housed 50 Jewish refugee families. It was set up like a *kibbutz*—a communal living arrangement where everyone was assigned jobs and shared the fruits of their labor. Money to pay for this food and other necessities was provided by *Bricha*, a Jewish relief organization, whose mission was to help Jewish refugees. In a way, it reminded me of the partisan camps where everything was shared. The difference was that now we weren't in danger, we weren't hungry or cold, we had friends, and we finally had hope for the future.

For some reason, the Germans had not occupied Turda, so its Jewish community had not been subjected to Nazi cruelty. These Jews hadn't lost their homes and jobs or been forced into a ghetto. They were well aware of their good fortune and were deeply sympathetic to survivors. They generously gave us money, food, clothes, and small housewarming gifts. They were particularly impressed that Papa was a doctor, and often invited us for *Shabbat* dinners in their own homes.[13]

Much to our surprise and relief, the local Gentiles were completely different from those we'd encountered in Poland and Hungary. They were *not* antisemitic! There were no restrictions on where we could go, and we didn't have to be afraid of bullies calling us names and throwing rocks at us, so we moved freely throughout the town. One of my favorite places was Turda's wonderful

13 *Shabbat* is the Jewish religious service held at sundown on Friday night, to mark the beginning of the Sabbath—Saturday—the Jewish day of rest.

bakery—how I wish I could once again taste their glorious pastries! I also enjoyed going to the movies. I saw every movie that played there—some I saw several times! I worked really hard to learn the Romanian language so I could understand the dialogue.

The residents of the compound were involved in lots of interesting activities—it was like a 24-hour Jewish Community Center. I especially loved their musical productions. Locals enjoyed coming to our performances so there was always an appreciative audience. Somehow, I got the idea that I should sing in the upcoming show. I carefully practiced an old Yiddish lullaby that I remembered my grandparents singing to me: *"Raisins and Almonds."* Here are the sweet lyrics:

Raisins and Almonds *(Traditional Yiddish Lullaby)*

In the corner of the temple school
Sits a widowed daughter of Zion
Rocking her only son, in a little cradle, to sleep
And sings to him a tender lullaby
Under Yidele's (little Jew's) cradle
Stands a snow white little goat
That will be taken to market
That will be Yidele's calling too
Trading in raisins and almonds
So sleep now Yidele sleep

The night of my performance, I was nervous, but I was used to acting brave and ignoring my anxiety, so I stood up straight, took a big breath, and put everything I had into that tune. I was rewarded by thunderous applause, and I felt mature and proud of my achievement. After the show, people crowded around me, giving me hugs and kisses, tearfully telling me how much my song had touched their hearts, and how beautifully I had sung it. One of them, an elderly Jewish woman, must have felt sorry for me, because she took my hand and pressed some money into it. Of course, today I know she meant well, I probably reminded her of a beloved lost child, but that night, her act of kindness made me feel like a street beggar receiving a donation for singing my song.

While we were lucky to find this place of safety, the living conditions became quite challenging. We all shared a communal kitchen and the adults rotated cooking responsibilities. We all ate together, and also shared the laundry, lavatories, and every area except for the small rooms where we slept. So the only privacy we had was when we were sleeping. My parents were not happy with this lack of privacy, and it didn't take them long to decide to use some of their few remaining gold coins to rent a small room of our own in another family's apartment in town. Since we had almost no belongings, we moved in quickly.

Once we'd settled into our room, our days took on a pleasant routine. But as usual, just when life finally seemed to be getting normal, something bad happened. During the time we'd been with the partisans, Papa had developed a painful hernia. This happens when part of an intestine pokes through an opening in the muscle that holds it in place, and creates a lump or bubble.

Papa's condition had worsened to the point where the pain was unbearable. He knew it would only get worse unless he had surgery. The closest place where this operation could be performed was in Cluj, Romania, a larger city about 30 miles away. Papa couldn't go without Mama to take care of him afterwards, and neither of them wanted to leave me with friends in Turda, so we all packed some clothes and left for Cluj. We rented a room there during the three weeks Papa was recovering in the hospital.

Again as usual, when something bad happened, another bad thing soon followed. After Papa had been discharged from the hospital, we were looking forward to returning to the comforts of Turda, but we were surprised by bad news. The Soviets had now invaded Romania. So there we were, in the wrong place at the wrong time. Again. And we needed to get out of Romania—fast. But first we had to go back to Turda to pack up our recently acquired belongings.

Chapter 12
November 1945-April 1946: *Wandering Jews*

We tried to keep Papa as comfortable as possible on the train ride back to Turda. Once we'd gotten to our apartment, he rested while Mama and I packed up our few belongings. Then, without a second look, we hustled right back to the train station. Leaving a place had become more common than actually living somewhere, and even though we'd been happy in Turda, our reality didn't provide opportunities for us to get attached to places.

In the short time that we had been away from the station, it had grown chaotic with crowds of people trying to leave Turda. It seemed as if everyone was trying to get away. Adding to the confusion were the pets and small farm animals that people were taking. And since it was a hot summer day, the stench of frightened, sweating humans, and noisy, dirty animals—who weren't particular about where they went to the bathroom—was overwhelming.

Once on board, we managed to snag three seats together, with Papa near the window, so he wouldn't get jostled. And we braced ourselves for the trip back to—of all places—Budapest! It really made no sense to me that we would be leaving Turda to escape the coming Soviets, only to go back to Soviet-controlled Budapest, which we'd left because it was so miserable. Just as I was trying to figure this out, something really weird happened.

Out of nowhere, a group of tough-looking armed Soviet soldiers stormed aboard and kicked us all off the train. Mama and I stuck to Papa's sides, trying to protect him from what had become a rough, angry crowd. The soldiers had taken over the train because they needed to get to Budapest. At that point, we were tired of being pushed around, and decided that nothing was going to stop us. So, even with Papa in such fragile condition, we—and many others—decided to climb, along with our belongings, up onto the roof of the train! It probably would have looked funny if we hadn't been so panic-stricken. All these terrified, yet determined, people carrying crying babies, bulging suitcases, food baskets, and frightened animals, trying desperately to scramble to the top of train cars. Once we go on the top, we carefully jockeyed for space, trying not to make anyone angry. We definitely did not want to get shoved off!

So there we were, the three of us, huddled together, about to ride on the roof of a speeding train car from Turda, Romania to Budapest, Hungary—300 miles. In the wind. Under the brutal summer sun. Or thunder storms. Day and night. Mama and I did our best to adjust to this new challenge, sitting on either side of Papa to keep him as safe as possible. We expected the train to leave any minute. But it didn't. So we waited. And we waited some more. And then, thinking our situation couldn't get any worse, the Soviets started yelling at us to climb down from the train. Now what? So with heavy hearts, heavy suitcases, and a very weakened Papa, the three of us awkwardly made our way back to the ground. The crowd was in such a fury that I feared the Soviets would just shoot us all.

For some reason, however, they not only didn't shoot us, but they decided to allow us to use two train cars. Apparently they weren't in the mood for a riot. Of course the two train cars could not hold all the people, so further chaos erupted. Amidst the frantic crowd, we just barely managed to squeeze back on board. The heat was unbearable, and some of the people who'd gotten on ahead of us, had fainted. So mounds of fallen people, their animals, and possessions filled the narrow aisles. Knowing that this would not end well, Papa gathered all of his strength and spirit, made his way off the train, and trying to look strong and important, approached a car filled with Soviet military officers.

Mama and I held our breath, watching him through the window, and hoping he wouldn't get hurt, arrested, or killed. Summoning up his best conversational Russian and a friendly smile, Papa introduced himself as Dr. Miasnik, adding that he was a surgeon who had served with the Soviet partisans in Belorussia. He inquired, "Perhaps you heard of the hospital we built in the Lipiczany forest?" And luckily for us, they *had* heard of him—and the hospital! The officers were highly impressed both by Papa's faultless Russian, and his service alongside the Soviets against the Germans. They slapped him on the back—fortunately not too hard, and called him, "Comrade Dr. Miasnik." Then they welcomed him to join them in their own comfortable car. And just as he had done in Lida, when the partisans first came to take him to the forest, Papa informed the officers that his wife and daughter must come along with him. Again, luckily for us, the Soviet officers extended their welcome to us!

So instead of suffering on the top of a train, or being crowded into a 2nd class car with other refugees, we traveled to Budapest in comfort and luxury, with "friendly" companions. Just as when we shared a train car with Soviets traveling from Szczuczyn to Lublin, these soldiers insisted on sharing their wonderful food with us, and we all told stories and sang patriotic songs together. Except for having to be careful not to make them angry, it almost felt like a party. So once again we'd gone from being abused by the Soviets to being their guests. These two experiences with Soviet soldiers in train cars provided an extreme contrast with my experiences living under their harsh control. And as I watched their drunken faces, and listened to their raucous laughter, I understood for the first time how thin the line is between normalcy and horror.

Unbeknownst to us, while we were blissfully enjoying the benefits of our comfortable trip, just over our heads, an unspeakable disaster had come to many innocent people. Apparently, after the Soviets were all safely settled in their cozy train cars, hundreds of desperate people had decided to risk riding on the train car roofs. They couldn't have imagined what would happen when the train went through a tunnel. And there were several tunnels on our route. It was only when we got off the train in Budapest, grateful for our safe and comfortable trip, that we heard the terrible stories about all the people who had snuck back onto the roof of the train.

Apparently, there's a powerful suction force that occurs when high-speed trains go through tunnels. These wretched, innocent people of all ages, many of whom had just barely survived so many atrocities, these brave and desperate people who were trying so hard not to give up, had actually been sucked off the train-car and slammed into the tunnel walls. Many then fell on the tracks under the train. Sickened by this terrible news, I realized how close we'd come to a hideous death, and that we owed our lives to those Soviet soldiers—and Papa's courage.

Once again, an agency helped find us a place to live. Once again, we slept on the crowded floor of a refugee-filled apartment building. Once again, we didn't have enough food, bathrooms, privacy, or other basics of daily life. And just as we'd feared, Budapest wasn't any better this time than it was the last time. We were miserable. Of course, as always, Mama and Papa were busy planning our next move—and within a week we were on yet another train.

And this time we had an entirely new destination: Graz, Austria. While we were fortunate to have false identification papers, we were not so fortunate in terms of money. Other than a few gold coins, we had no cash. Mama was tired of dragging her old, worn-out comforter around Europe, so it made sense for her to sell it. We now had enough cash to last for a week. The comforter had saved us one last time.

As we traveled across Europe, I was struck by how some areas, were completely demolished, and some hadn't been touched. And I was especially interested to learn that some regions of Austria were now occupied by Soviets, while others were occupied by Americans or the British. I hoped with all my heart that we would be going a region that was far away from the Soviets. We really looked forward to our arrival in beautiful Austria.

Unfortunately, the Austrians were not looking forward to our arrival. In fact, the Austrians hated us. They wouldn't even look at us. They seemed to look right through us as if we were invisible. And on the occasions when they couldn't avoid seeing us, their faces twisted into expressions of hate and disgust as they hurled frightening insults at us. These Austrians resented us for still being alive. Can you imagine hating a 10-year old girl because she dared to live?

Again, an agency that helped displaced Jews found us a place to stay. And again, it was a miserably crowded, refugee-filled apartment. We stayed there for only a few days before beginning yet another journey. This time, along with some other survivors, we were being loaded onto three open trucks and taken to another region in Austria, which thankfully, was occupied by the British. We were nervous because our journey would take us through a mountainous area controlled by the Soviets. They could stop and send us back. Fortunately, the agency that was helping us had already bribed the Soviets along our route. Despite the bribe, however, we were stopped once by a Soviet soldier who gave us a hard time. Fortunately, a man in our group produced a precious bottle of vodka and gave it to the guard—and the issue was instantly resolved. After two days, we finally reached another very small town, and were finally free of the Soviets.

So here it was the summer of 1945, and I was ten years old. My parents and I had been on the run since September of 1939. Six years in the life of ten-year-old is a very long time, and I had missed all the important developmental stages and social experiences of childhood. The only three friendships I'd experienced, Tuska in Lida, Halinka in Szczuczyn, and the boy in Lublin, had all ended abruptly. So friendless, and rootless, it was as if we had become robots, moving from one crisis to the next. We'd been fleeing from one deadly enemy to another for such a long time that we were too exhausted to feel much of anything. Yes, we were relieved to be free of the Soviets and the Nazis. But even though we were safe, we didn't have anything resembling a home. Or much money—or anything left to sell.

In fact, all our possessions could easily—and quickly—be packed into two small backpacks. As if we were animals, only our basic needs—food, water, and shelter—were met in what were known as displaced persons (DP) camps. Human needs, such as making friends, were a luxury we couldn't afford. So despite always being surrounded by people, we were lonely. And unlike my parents, who at least had each other, I was a young girl—an only child—who longed to have a friend.

Adding to my sense of social isolation was the sad fact that despite everything we'd been through, Jewish refugees were not welcomed anywhere in Europe. We just moved around from one displaced persons' camp to another. Sometimes we were in buildings, sometimes we were in tents. We constantly had to adapt to whatever new situations arose. Our lives were totally controlled by the agencies that had been set up to help Jewish refugees. We had no idea if these people knew what they were doing. So yes, "freedom"—whatever that meant—was a great relief, but what good was freedom if we were still powerless over our own lives, and couldn't even imagine a future?

In the midst of constant change, and with the absence of accurate news from the outside world, one thing remained a constant: the endless rumors. Usually they were pretty much the same: We would soon be going to yet another camp. Someone was sick. Someone had died. Someone had gotten angry and started screaming at someone else. Someone had gotten fed up and run away. One day, the rumors included something new. We heard that our group would soon be going to Italy—wherever that was. Italy could have been up on the moon, for all I knew.

A few days later, we got a big surprise. Five large military trucks rumbled into our camp, bringing anxiety to all of us. The commander got out of his truck and using a hand-held loudspeaker, ordered us to pack up our things and climb into the back of one of the trucks. Nobody moved. We all just stared at the soldier—paralyzed by fear.

We all thought they were going to take us to prison camps—or kill us out in some forest. Totally defenseless, we stood there as if we'd suddenly been turned into statues. Seeing and understanding our fear, the commander smiled and told us we didn't have to be afraid. He then astonished us by explaining that the soldiers were Jews! Jewish soldiers! And they were part of something called the *Jewish Brigade of the British Army!*[14] These young, strong, handsome soldiers did their best to make us feel safe and comfortable. The fact that some of them spoke Yiddish was a welcome bonus. They consoled and encouraged us by telling us:

"Hot nit moiré." ("Don't be afraid.")
"Mir zainen Yidden." ("We are Jews.")
"Mir veln aich nemen mit unz." ("We will take you with us.")

The amazing sound of our beloved *Mamaloshen* (refers to Yiddish, the mother tongue or first language of Eastern European Jews) being spoken by Jewish soldiers gave us hope for the first time in six years. When they confirmed that the rumors we'd heard about going to Italy were true, and that they were going to take us there, we actually felt delight for the first time in six years! Eager to be on our way, we statues sprang to life and gathered our few belongings and climbed into a truck.

At sundown, the proud parade of five Jewish military trucks being driven by strong Jewish soldiers, and filled with newly energized and suddenly hopeful Jewish refugees, left the camp. The trip to a small military camp in northern Italy took all night, but I didn't sleep a wink. In fact, I stood up much of the time, unable to take my eyes off the beautiful scenery during the day, and then at night, the bright full moon, that seemed to be encouraging us on our way.

Upon our early morning arrival, we saw that this camp had tents, but no buildings. We realized that it wasn't a permanent camp. This allowed the soldiers to go where they were needed, set up camp, take care of refugees, and if necessary, pack up and go to another location. We were immediately taken to a roped off section at the edge of the camp, separated into groups of males and females, told to undress and leave our clothes in a pile so they could be disinfected. Then we were sprayed with a pesticide called *DDT*.[15] This embarrassing process was necessary to make sure no lice were living on our bodies and in our hair, but it made me feel as if we were animals trapped a pen. Then we washed ourselves with perfumed soap, and dried ourselves off with rough towels. Since our clothes hadn't dried yet, we wrapped ourselves in old bedsheets the soldiers

---

14   The British Army's Jewish Brigade was created in September 1944 to fight the Germans in Italy. After the war, the Brigade created and maintained displaced persons camps for Jewish survivors, and helped them emigrate to Palestine.

15   *DDT*: A chemical compound that not only kills lice, but as we learned years later, is also dangerous for the environment—as well as humans. It was banned in the US in 1972.

gave us. What a sight we must have been: a rag-tag bunch of refugees, wrapped in sheets, making our way around the tents. When our clothes had dried enough to put on, we got dressed and went to the dining tent to eat breakfast.

On the way into the tent, I spied the food they planned to serve us. It was something called *Spam* that I'd never seen before.[16] The strange-looking canned meat was gray and mushy, but we'd learned long ago that food was food—its appearance or taste didn't matter to us. We'd eaten all kinds of so-called food that looked and tasted awful. When I noticed that the food-serving process was going to take a while, I decided to step outside and enjoy the beautiful fresh, clean, spring air. Little did I know that I was in for a big surprise!

16 *Spam* is processed, cooked, and canned, pork that was used by the military during World War II because it was convenient and easy to carry.

Chapter 13

February-June 1946: *A Surprise Reunion!*

Even though it was cold outside, it was wonderful to be able to enjoy fresh air, without worrying about freezing to death. As I stood on the step outside the tent's door and looked around the camp, I felt a tremendous sense of joy to be free, safe, and living with Jewish soldiers. I took in deep blissful breaths, inhaling the air of freedom and safety. And then I almost choked.

Exiting a Jeep and walking directly toward me (actually, he was walking directly toward the dining tent) was a very tall and handsome soldier who for some reason caused my heart to jump. I felt a powerful connection to him. Somehow, in a flash, I recognized my father's first-cousin, Josel! Leaping off the step, I ran at him full speed with my arms waving wildly, screaming, "Josel! Josel! It's me! It's me, Mirele!" And then laughing and crying, I jumped into his surprised arms and hugged his neck with all my strength! Of course, he was flummoxed. Who could this wild-eyed creature hanging on to his neck be? Finally realizing who I was, he recovered fast, and hugged me close, crying, "Mirele, sweet little Mirele! Is it really you?" I nodded furiously against his face, crying, "Yes! Yes! It's me!" Next, he asked if my parents were alive. And just as I started to tell him they were alive and sitting safely inside the dining tent, they came outside looking for me.

Their shock at seeing their daughter in the arms of a crying soldier evaporated when they saw that it was Josel. They rushed to wrap us both in a huge hug, repeating his name. Josel exclaimed over and over, "Chaim, Bronka, Mirele, you are alive! Thank God! Alive!" Sobbing and hanging on tightly to each other, we managed to hobble back into the tent where our sumptuous Spam feast awaited us. Even though it was the first family meal of celebration in years, between the talking, the crying, and more hugging, we didn't eat much.

We listened raptly as Josel told us what had happened to him after the Germans invaded Lida. He'd immediately been drafted into the retreating Soviet Army, and shipped off into the central region of the Soviet Union, leaving his wife and two children. During the weeks that it took to get these new recruits to their Soviet base, Josel never stopped planning to escape, and somehow reunite with his family. He faced many challenges—not the least of which was what he'd eat and where he'd sleep while on the run. His first challenge was that deserting the Soviet Army would be difficult and could result in his execution. Second, even if he got away from the Soviets, he might be found and shot by Germans. Third, he knew he could not go back to Lida since it was now occupied by the Nazis. Fourth, he had no idea where his family might be.

Despite all these challenges, Josel still had somehow managed to get out of the USSR, elude the Germans, and get all the way through Turkey, on his way to Palestine. He found and joined some Jewish soldiers who belonged to the British Jewish Brigade and were on the way to Italy to fight the Nazis. When Italy was liberated, Josel resumed his search for his family. He went from one DP camp to another, always asking if anyone had made contact with Lida survivors. He was horrified to learn of the Lida Massacre, but never gave up the hope that his family had somehow survived. At this point in the conversation, with tears streaming down his face, Papa took Josel's hand and barely able to speak, told him that his precious wife and children had died during the Lida ghetto massacre. Bowing his head, and holding Papa's hand tightly, Josel's body shook as he sobbed silently for his murdered wife and children.

After hearing this tragic news, Josel became determined to ensure that his only living relatives would have a better life. Because we were in a camp run by Jewish soldiers, Josel went to the commander and told him in Hebrew that my father was his long-lost brother. He explained what we all had gone through. When Josel informed the commander that he would now be moving us from this camp and taking us to his own camp in Mestre, the teary-eyed commander shook his hand, congratulated him on finding his brother, and wished us all well. Once again, we were on our way—but this time, our destination would be wonderful beyond our wildest imaginations!

This was because instead of moving us directly onto his military base in Mestre, Josel arranged for us to spend some time in the beautiful, world-renown beachfront resort area of *Lido di Venezia* on the Adriatic Sea. Somehow, he knew that we needed a wonderful vacation as a way of transitioning back to normal life. Fortunately, since Jewish soldiers were stationed there, Josel would be able to stay with us.

The Lido was an island off the coast of Venice. We could only get there by taking an hour-long ferry boat ride. I was beside myself with excitement! Other than in pictures, I'd never seen a boat, much less been in one! I'd never seen a beach! And for sure, I'd never seen the Adriatic Sea! It was a beautiful sunny day, and I felt as if I'd entered the magical land of a fairy tale. I gazed in breathless wonder at the sparkling blue Adriatic Sea, whose glistening waves swelled and rolled softly all the way to the horizon.

The beautiful port of Lido di Venezia was filled with boats coming and going, and I was particularly fascinated by the graceful sail boats. As soon as we disembarked, we began walking straight towards the beach as if hypnotized. With each step, we became more and more excited! Close to the water's edge, we sat in the sand, and as if we were at an exciting movie, watched the turquoise waves that now gently rolled onto the shore. Since there'd been no tourists during or immediately after the war, there were few people on the beach, and it seemed as if it all belonged to us.

Eventually, when the sun had set and we'd grown hungry, we tore ourselves away from this fantasyland of sand and sea, and followed Josel to our new "home." It would be an understatement to say I was stunned when I saw it. Before the war, this elaborately designed and decorated building that faced the sea had been an opulent hotel for wealthy tourists.

Although we were definitely tourists of a different kind, we were welcomed by military staff as if we were royalty. This was because they knew my father was a hero. We were shown to a fancy penthouse on the top floor, where the view from every window was breathtaking. My parents were given clean military clothing, but since there were no clothes for children, I just wore my own. Thanks to the military laundry, however, my old clothes were cleaner than ever! The soldiers gave us little gifts, as well as whatever soaps, toothpaste, shampoo, and other personal items we might need. All we had to do was ask, and our every request was instantly fulfilled. We had suddenly gone from being impoverished, stateless refugees, shuttling around from one DP or army camp to another, to living in the lap of luxury!

My parents couldn't wait to take showers in the luxurious bathroom, and wrap themselves up in the fluffy white towels. This was all so new to me that at first, I wasn't sure about taking a shower, but once I got in, I never wanted to get out! I stood under the warm streaming water until my parents insisted I leave my watery paradise so we could go to dinner. Downstairs, in the very charming, elegant dining room, we were served as much mouth-watering food as we could eat—each dish more delightful than the last—and best of all, there was no Spam in sight!

Unfortunately, since Josel wasn't an officer, he wasn't able to share in our royal circumstances. Instead, he and his buddies were housed and fed in a far less elegant section of the hotel, where the hotel staff used to live. We felt sad that his living arrangements were less luxurious than ours, but we knew he took great joy in seeing us finally being treated so well.

During our stay in Lido di Venezia, my parents and I took full advantage of the beach, rarely missing a day of fun playing in the sand and wading the water. I didn't have a bathing suit, so I wore my best panties. Swirling in the clear turquoise water, I felt as if the filth from my time in the forest was finally being washed off. I'd never felt so clean! Or so carefree.

I was still lonely, however, because even though there were other children playing nearby, I didn't approach them. I didn't feel comfortable with other children. I wasn't sure I'd even know how to play with them. I sensed that my experiences had made me so different from them that they would not accept me.

Photo of Mama, Josel, and another of the Jewish soldiers in the British Brigade. Venice, Italy: 1946.

What children would believe me if I told them of my past?

After one wondrous, unforgettable week at the beach, our vacation came to an end. Feeling refreshed and hopeful about the future, we went with Josel to his military base at Mestre. Other refugee families had also moved there, so we weren't the only civilians. Again, even though there were a few children, none of us bonded. I think they probably felt the same way I did about the pain of friendships. The pain of loss. Even though we no lon-

With Mama and Papa, Venice, Italy: 1946

ger lived in luxury, our room and food were just fine for us—and far better than in the other places we'd been forced to live. The soldiers treated us as if we were heroes, and they were eager to hear about our experiences in the partisans—especially Papa's medical work in the forest. Their reactions alternated between anger at what we'd been through, and admiration at how we'd dealt with our circumstances.

But we weren't the only ones telling stories. These Jewish soldiers had plenty to tell us about the Jewish homeland, they referred to as *Eretz Israel*, which was currently controlled by the British. I was fascinated by their tales of Jewish *kibbutzim*—farms where free, strong, dedicated Jews owned and shared the land together—collectively. They worked together as teams to turn the vast desert into lush irrigated acres of fruits, vegetables, and trees. I hungered for more stories about these fearless, hardworking Jews who were living, working, and succeeding in their own ancient homeland. *Our* own ancient Jewish homeland. And I wanted to go there and be part of this new land. Even though I didn't know the word yet, I was becoming a *Zionist*.[17] I marveled when the soldiers told me that in Palestine, children were highly valued and "welcomed with open arms." And that children were treasured because they represented the future. And so I finally began to dream of a future—a future where my parents and I would live in freedom in this glorious Jewish land.

17 The *Zionist* movement originated in 1897 for the purpose of re-establishing a Jewish nation in Palestine. Part of this region became Israel in 1948.

But in the meantime, we needed to learn to live as free people who could support ourselves in Venice. Papa was not the kind of person to waste time, so he quickly began providing medical care to the other refugees. He carefully saved whatever they were able to pay him, and after a couple of months, he had saved enough money for us to move from the military base into an apartment in Venice. Papa arranged for us to rent a room on the third-floor in a private home. It was owned by a kind Italian woman and her son, who coincidentally, was a medical student. We had kitchen privileges, so Mama and the Italian lady shared some of the cooking—as well as each other's recipes. Sometimes we ate in a dining room of Jewish soldiers who were stationed near us in Venice. It was wonderful to spend time with these lively and strong Jewish soldiers, and I never tired of hearing about our Jewish homeland. They reminded me of Josel, and made me feel as if I were part of a huge Jewish family.

Living with the Italian family was a whole new and very welcome experience for me. I was surrounded by beauty and a joy for life I hadn't known existed. The house was filled with warm affection, music, dancing, laughter, and the ever-present aromas of delicious food. We did our best to communicate despite the language barrier—and it was amazing how well hand gestures and facial expressions could convey our thoughts. Outside the house, there was even more music, and food, as well as endless activities such as outdoor opera, concerts, and a strange game called, *Bocci Ball*.[18] Even in the middle of the night, people would be out in the streets singing songs from operas. And they all sounded like professional singers! What impressed me the most, however, was that there was absolutely no trace of antisemitism in Venice. Everyone was friendly to us, and the adults acted as if every child they saw—even me—was their own child.

We saw Josel often, and he became important in my life. He always brought gifts of clothing and chocolate for me, and more importantly, he filled in an empty space left by my father who was now always working. I know Josel saw in me the opportunity to be a loving father figure—a role he'd been unable to fulfill for his own children. He also had a great sense of humor, and always knew how to make me laugh when I was sad. And if I was nervous, all I had to do was jump into his arms—just like I had the day I saw him at the army camp—and I would feel safe and protected.

Adding strength to our relationship was his pride in my becoming a Zionist. He loved watching my eyes glow as he told me stories about his beloved Palestine, and its heroic people. *Our* heroic people. Sadly, for me,

---

18 *Bocci Ball* is an outdoor game similar to bowling. It is popular in Italy.

just a few months after we'd moved in with the Italians, Josel's military unit was ordered to return to Palestine. Even though he was thrilled to return to the Jewish homeland, this was a devastating blow to both of us. We'd each experienced the traumatic loss of loved ones, and all too often, a separation became permanent.

At the end of our last day together, I sobbed my heart out, hanging on tightly to Josel's neck, reliving my last day with my beloved grandparents. He tried to soothe me with some jokes, but for the first time, he couldn't make me laugh. And even being in his arms did not make me feel safe. He spoke softly to me saying,

"Mirele, sweetheart, please cheer up. We will be together soon in Tel Aviv. I'll be there when you arrive, and I'll show you all of Palestine! We'll walk through orange groves and go to the most beautiful beach in the world! You'll walk where our ancestors walked. Shalom, precious Mirele, I love you."

Needless to say, I completely fell apart. It seemed as if I would never have a relationship that didn't end. Every time I opened my heart to someone, I ended up with a broken heart.

My loneliness became even more heart-wrenching when we went to Shabbat services in a synagogue for the first time since before the war. Fortunately, unlike so many other European cities, Venice had not been badly damaged during the war. Unlike so many other Jewish buildings, the war had not harmed the magnificent, centuries old synagogue. The richness of Jewish culture—a richness I had no memory of, and which had been all but extinguished throughout Europe, was all there welcoming us. The intricate beauty of the elaborate architecture was hypnotic, and almost overwhelming to me. I was surprised to see many people I already knew from the Jewish refugee community as well as many Italian Jews. We all seemed to be connected and filled with love for each other—as if we were one huge family so grateful to be reuniting.

For those of us who were refugees, however, our joy at being surrounded by Jews in a beautiful synagogue was bittersweet. Foremost on our minds was the nightmare we'd been through, and the loss of our loved ones. As we sat there, filled with such intense emotions, the chanting of ancient—yet still familiar—prayers filled our ears and our hearts. But soon these sounds faded into the background as all three of us began weeping at the same time. It was as if the chanting opened long-locked gates to our hearts, releasing the pain and sorrow of the last seven years.

Flooded with memories, we were unable to speak. Finally, Mama put her arms around me and asked why I was crying. In a breaking voice, I managed to reply, "I'm crying for Aunt Ala. Missing her hurts so much." Drying my tears with her handkerchief, Mama told me she felt the same way. She ached for her lost sister. And her brother. And her parents. And all her aunts, uncles, cousins, and friends. We prayed even harder that night for the survival of our loved ones.

Starting the next day, Mama wasted no time turning our prayers in to action. She began a frenzied letter-writing campaign to her brothers in America, hoping that their addresses hadn't changed. Determined to let them know we had survived, and were safe in Venice, she wrote letters every day, hoping at least one would get through. It took quite a while for mail to arrive during those days—sometimes even weeks. Letters to and from America took the longest time, but eventually, we started receiving responses from Mama's brothers.

Every time the mailman came, I could hardly contain my excitement, knowing that he would be bringing packages of exotic canned food, beautiful clothing, and other special gifts for me. I gazed in wonder at the photos of so many healthy, good-looking relatives that I'd never met—all of whom were waiting for us to join them in America. They would sponsor us and provide us with a place to live as well as jobs for my parents. What could be more perfect?

Unfortunately, this upcoming perfect future caused me to experience extremely mixed emotions. This was because I planned to go to Palestine—not America. And of course, my plan included my parents. Josel was waiting in Palestine for us all. He'd already lost one family—how could we abandon him by going to America? As usual, I knew better than to give voice to my emotions, and I buried them along with all the others. Unable to share wholeheartedly in my parents' joy, I resigned myself to pretending to be happy. By that time, I no longer expected to ever be happy.

But as sometimes had happened before, I was in for a surprise. And this time—for a change—the surprise was a good one. Her name was Eva.

Chapter 14

July-September 1946: *Hellos and Goodbyes in Italy*

Imagine what a gorgeous, vibrant city like Venice would have looked and felt like to me at that stage of my life! In a very short space of time I had gone from being a terrified, starving, lonely little Polish Jewish girl, who had barely survived the Nazis, to a nervous Polish Jewish girl who'd barely escaped the Soviets. Life in a mosquito-infested swamp or a refugee camp, was far more familiar than life in the breathtaking architecture of one of the world's most beautiful cities. Nothing in my vivid imagination could have conjured up a fantasy as spectacular as Venice.

I was fascinated to learn that Venice was founded in 400 AD by the Romans on a chain of over 100 islands. Its 150 winding canals were always busy with *gondolas* (traditional, flat-bottomed Venetian rowing boats), as well as *vaporetti* (motorized water-buses), and ferry-boats. Its more than 400 bridges bustled with pedestrians. I was dazzled by its manicured gardens and lush parks, along with its endless bridges, cafes, churches, theaters, museums, and sophisticated shops. I didn't know it then, but Venice also had a long Jewish history. Jewish traders had done business in Venice as early as the 900s, and Jews have lived in Venice since the Middle Ages. In fact, the word, "ghetto," with which I was already very sadly familiar, is said to have originated in Venice.

Another benefit of living in Venice among Jewish refugees was that one of them was a pretty Hungarian Jewish girl, who became the friend I'd always longed for. Along with her parents, grandmother, and little brother, Eva had managed to survive the Nazis. After the war, her family also had not been happy living under Communist control. So like us, they had gone from city to city, and camp to camp, until they too were helped by the Jewish Brigade, and ended up in Venice.

As pre-teens who had been friendless for most of our lives, the ache of loneliness had profoundly affected us. We each craved a loving, loyal, and trustworthy friend—someone we could tell our secrets to. Someone who understood our painful past, as well as our dreams. Someone who wouldn't disappear in the middle of the night . . . someone we wouldn't have to leave without a goodbye. Our meeting was the answer to both of our prayers, and our connection was immediate and intense.

Unlike so many other Jewish children who had perished in Nazi Occupied Europe, Eva and I had managed to survive the Germans. In the process of surviving, however, we'd had to put our emotions on hold. We'd never had the chance to really think about, much less talk about, the horrors we were experiencing. We'd had to function as robots, doing whatever was necessary to survive. Thinking about our losses or getting emotional about our reality would have interfered with our ability to survive. Now that we were safe and

St Mark's Basilica, Venice, Italy

had found each other, our friendship became the most important thing in our young worlds. And since we weren't enrolled in school, we were able to spend a lot of time together.

Along with so many others, Eva and I both had become enthusiastic Zionists, and dreamed of living on a kibbutz in Palestine. We were eager to learn Hebrew words and phrases from the Jewish soldiers, and we were excited to sing and dance to Israeli music. Even though we were only eleven, our parents let us explore Venice on our own. And post-World War II Venice provided the perfect setting for two young and very curious Jewish refugees!

There never was a dull moment as Eva and I investigated the quaint streets around the canals, and if we were really lucky, someone would buy us tickets for gondola rides. We window-shopped at the fancy stores on the *Rialto Bridge*,[19] and visited the *Piazza di San Marco*[20] listening to its melodious cathedral bells. We squeezed through tiny, mysterious alleys that barely had room for two people. Our winter in Venice was especially rainy, and the canals often overflowed. This probably irritated the adults, but Eva and loved wading and splashing in the water.

We would often sit on the edge of a canal, watching the gondolas and vaporetti come and go, and sharing stories about our wartime experiences. Eva cracked up when I told her I'd received a gun for my ninth birthday. She rolled her eyes and said she would have loved to see me looking like a tough little boy with a shaved head and a gun.

Somehow, we were able to laugh even at the most painful events. As young girls who had never been children, we were mesmerized by the sight of what seemed to be normal families doing normal family things—without having to worry about being shot. Little kids just being silly instead of worrying that Nazi soldiers would grab them. Parents yelling at children who were misbehaving—without having to worry that they'd be taken to a concentration camp. Big brothers showing younger siblings how to turn cartwheels or fly a kite . . . or sitting on a park bench on a sunny day, secure in the knowledge that there would be a tomorrow.

For the first time in our lives, Eva and I could act like normal 11-year-olds. We weren't on the run. We didn't have to always be on the alert. We didn't have

---

19   The *Rialto Bridge*, which crosses the Grand Canal in Venice, was built in the late 1500s, and is often described as "the true heart of Venice." It is still supported by approximately 12,000 wooden pilings upon which it was built over 400 years ago. Photo: Damiano Baschiera #633093 on Unsplash

20   *Piazza San Marco* is a beautiful open-air plaza in the heart of Venice, that was created in the 9th century, and paved in the 1200s. Two of the famous buildings that surround this plaza include *St Mark's Basilica,* and the *Doge's Palace.*

to be quiet. We weren't always hungry. We didn't have to eat disgusting so-called food, and be grateful to have it. We could be silly! And best of all, we were able to share our long-buried feelings with someone who understood them. We'd both experienced painful losses of beloved family and friends—losses made even more painful by the absence of goodbye hugs. I told Eva about my little friend, Tuska, in the Lida ghetto, and Halinka in Szczuczyn. Eva was especially interested in my stories about my sweet first love in Lublin.

While we had a lot of experiences in common, however, there was one big difference. Since the Germans had occupied Poland in September 1941, and Hungary not until March 1944, Eva had had the chance to attend school before the Germans came. I hadn't had that chance. She was far more academically accomplished than I was, and sometimes I felt inferior to her. Sensing my sadness, Eva always told me how much she admired my courage and spirit—and my "street smarts."

My close friendship with Eva was especially important because my relationship with my parents had begun to change. As a very young, only child during the war years, my connection with my parents had been absolute. My ability to instantly follow their orders determined whether I would live or die. There had been no time for deep discussions or introspection. I'd had to keep my thoughts and emotions buried deeply. Mama and Papa also had had to put their thoughts and emotions aside in order to focus on surviving and protecting me.

My parents were still a young couple, and had their own needs that had been postponed for too long. Living in Venice gave them the opportunity to make up for lost time—and they seemed to be off in their own little world, enjoying every minute. At this point in our lives, without the intensity of war, we didn't seem to need each other as much, and I felt a strange sense of separation from them. This was painful to me because despite having never belonged anywhere, I had at least always belonged to my parents. So now, I felt even more alone than ever. Eva filled the aching, empty space in my heart.

I would have been thrilled to continue my magical life in Venice forever, but this was not to be. The Jewish Relief agency that had been providing services for displaced Holocaust refugees had never planned for us all to stay in Venice. It was just a temporary stop on the way to either Palestine the USA, Canada, or a few other countries that had agreed to take Jewish survivors. So after ten months, they'd arranged for us to move to Rome. This end to my first experience with normal life, was made less difficult for me, because Eva and her family were also part of the group going to Rome. So despite our sadness about leaving Venice, we looked forward to our upcoming adventures in Rome.

Our group traveled in five big military trucks, and we were protected by armed, highly trained members of the Jewish Brigade. Eva and I were disappointed that we weren't able to travel in the same truck. After a hot, bumpy 5 1/2-hour trip through the gorgeous Italian countryside, we arrived at our destination: a luxurious private estate in the mountains just outside of Rome. When the huge iron gate of Monte Mario at 85 Camelluccia Street opened for us, I had no idea what to expect. Once the the gate had closed behind us, however, I thought I'd entered a new world. All we could see were, beautifully manicured trees and shrubs. Our parade of dusty army trucks provided a stark contrast to the beauty of the long, winding, tree-lined drive. We were stunned when a mansion suddenly appeared as if in a Hollywood movie.

Naturally, my curiosity was aroused, so I asked a lot of questions. It turns out that the Italian government had allowed Bricha to take over this vast, lush, 50-acre estate in order to create a kibbutz. Jewish Holocaust refugees would live, work, and play together communally, just like members of a real kibbutz in Palestine. In so doing, survivors would be preparing for their eventual return to the Jewish homeland in what was still known as Palestine.

Adding to my joy was that for the first time, I would actually have my own room. Of course it was not much bigger than a small closet, but it was mine—and I'd finally have some privacy! I'm sure my parents were thinking the same thing. Most of the other families had larger rooms, but they had to share them with other families. Unlike so many of the kibbutzim in Palestine, which were on farms in the desert, our first real kibbutz was housed on a luxury estate!

Once we'd gone to our rooms and cleaned up, Eva and I found each other and proceeded to explore every nook and cranny of the mansion and as much of the 50 acres as we could get to. As the days went by, we also explored the countryside surrounding the estate. We were pretty much free to go and do whatever we wanted. We ran through fruit orchards and ate our fill of oranges, apples, figs, dates, grapes, and persimmons—whatever was ripe!

In the weeks that followed, we played with and organized activities for the younger children. It was fun being one of the older kids and having the others look up to us. We understood all too well that these little ones had never had real childhoods. Other than Eva, none of us had gone to school, played with neighborhood friends, or gone to birthday parties—and we'd all been trained to trust no one and to fear strangers. Unlike our parents, we didn't even know what "home" meant. So despite our own lack of childhoods or having lived in family homes, Eva and I did the best we could to create a homelike atmosphere for the younger kids.

All the children at the Monte Mario kibbutz. I am the third person from the right, and Eva is the fifth person from the right: 1947

One of our first projects was to put on an outdoor musical show—in Yiddish! We put wooden boards together to make a stage, but we didn't have a curtain. I once again sang *"Raisins and Almonds,"* as I had in Romania, and was delighted to receive the same appreciative response from the audience. The younger children also sang Yiddish or Hebrew songs. We all danced some *Horas*,[21] and several children recited poems they had been taught. All the members of our kibbutz were in attendance, and they clapped loudly after each presentation. Eva and I were overjoyed and proud of our show and our little performers.

In addition to our own activities, there was always something exciting going on. People were always coming and going, and sometimes we even knew some of them from our days in the partisans or Turda. Among them were Dr. Rosenzweig, his wife, Sima, and their baby son, Nachum. Dr. Rosenzweig had worked with my father at the partisan hospital in the forest. Sima had been one of the nurses who helped them. Just like most of the residents in our villa kibbutz, the Rosenzweigs were planning to go to Palestine. They believed it was the only place where Jews would be free and safe. He was pleased that Eva and I planned to go, and kindly gave us, along with the younger children, Hebrew

21 The *Horah* is a Jewish circle dance typically accompanied by the tune, *Hava Nagila*, which means, *Let Us Rejoice!* It is traditionally danced at Jewish weddings and other joyous occasions.

lessons, including songs and dances, so that we'd feel at home when we moved to Palestine. So now I was speaking Polish and Yiddish with my parents, Yiddish with Eva, Italian with any Italians I met outside the villa, a bit of Russian and Romanian when the opportunities arose, and Hebrew every chance I got!

The kibbutz did not have a school, and my parents worried that I was missing out on an education. So in order to prepare me to attend a local public school, they hired a tutor to teach me how to read and write in Italian. Papa taught me arithmetic, while Mama taught me and biology, and used Polish text books to teach me geography. It was fun using maps to learn about the other countries that we'd lived in or traveled through. I especially enjoyed planning trips to places I hoped to visit in the future. Of course I wanted to learn as much as possible about Israel, which was then under British control. I also loved learning the names of the cities and states in the USA. They seemed long and almost nonsensical. Boston, Massachusetts. Sacramento, California, Tallahassee, Florida. Little did I know then, that within 18 months, I'd be living in a place called Brooklyn, New York!

As a result of my fascination with geography, I took up my first hobby, and became an avid stamp collector. One of the highlights of my day was the arrival of the postman, who always brought letters from my uncles in America. I prized the stamps on the envelopes. Eva did the same thing, and we also asked other residents of the kibbutz to give us stamps that came on their families' letters from other countries. So in a short time,

With Mama and Papa at Monte Mario kibbutz near Rome:1947

she and I had our own large collections. We played games with the stamps, and traded with each other. It reminded me of the terrible days when I'd played similar games and traded labels with Tuska in Lida. Good thing that Eva and I didn't have to go through garbage to find our stamps.

The days and weeks passed in a flurry of activities, and I began to look forward to my eleventh birthday. This year, even though there were no birthday parties in the kibbutz, my parents took me on a wonderful trip to a stamp store in Venice. They bought me some special stamps and a beautiful album to put them in.

I didn't expect anything from Eva—her friendship was the only present I needed. She did however, surprise me with a gift I treasured: a fancy little notebook in which she had written a lovely poem that I have never forgotten:

What shall I tell you
What shall I give you
I have such a short life myself
I have a heart that cares and feels
I love you, Miriam
That is all I can say

Our friendship continued to grow and deepen, as we shared more experiences together, crying and laughing ourselves silly. Because I was now older, the relationship was deeper than my previous wartime friendships. And because I now knew how to hope, my hopes for the future included Eva.

August 1946, was so brutally hot that we couldn't even go barefoot without blistering the bottoms of our feet. There were days when even breathing the hot air felt dangerous. The heat took away our energy and we spent most of our time laying in the grass under shady trees, hoping for a cool breeze.

No one had air-conditioning, so the only way to get real relief was to go to the beach. Fortunately, the kibbutz had a truck, so some of us kids would pile in, and one of the adults would drive us to the beach at Ostia. Unfortunately, everyone else had the same idea, so the beach was too crowded to enjoy. We did manage to squeeze in between some of the other people, and do a little wading in the water before giving up and going home.

The merciless heat continued for the rest of the week, and Eva seemed to lose even more energy. Right before my eyes, she seemed to grow weaker and weaker. I couldn't even get her to laugh at my silliest jokes and funny faces. And then, in spite of the heat she became ice cold. While most of us just wanted to take our clothes off, she shivered and needed blankets. And then she got hot and sweaty and threw the blankets off. She felt sick, and was in a lot of pain. When her worried parents took her temperature, they were alarmed to see that she was running a high fever—and it kept going higher.

Despite my parent's insistence that I stay away from her because I might also get sick, I spent all my waking hours in her room. And if there were no adults around, I sat right next to her on her bed. When she got the chills in spite of the heat, I'd lay down next to her and wrap my arms around her to provide some warmth. Painful memories of laying next to Mama in the zemlyanka, crying and begging her to get well filled my head with anxiety. Just as with Mama, I spoke softly to Eva, hoping that if I could just talk enough, my words would give her the strength to survive. I recounted all of our adventures—at first with words, and then with sobs...

"Eva, remember when we got lost in that little street by the canal?" "Eva, remember when we threw-up because we'd never seen figs before and we ate too many? Eva, remember how cute the little kids were in the musical show?" "Eva, remember splashing around in the streets when the canals flooded?" "Eva, please, please, please get better. We're going to Palestine soon. We'll be pioneers in the Jewish homeland. Your Hebrew name will be Chava, and you'll be my Chavele. Please, Eva, don't leave me."

But all my words, and all my love couldn't make Eva better. She just kept getting worse, and then the doctor told us the words we did not want to hear: Our sweet Eva had polio.[22] No one was sure what caused her illness but this merciless disease seemed to target children. On August 11, 1946, only a week after we'd gone to the beach to cool off, the unthinkable happened: my Eva died.

And my lovely, but fragile, world fell apart. I couldn't stop sobbing, and when there were no more tears, my body kept spasming. I couldn't comprehend that she was gone, that we wouldn't be giggling and going on adventures. That we wouldn't be going to Palestine. That we wouldn't be going anywhere or doing anything... because there was no more "we." The next day, I spent every minute I could with her mother and brother—we held onto each other crying hour after hour. But something worse was yet to come.

Eva would be having a funeral, and although I'd seen a lot of hideous deaths, I'd never been to a funeral. Standing at the gravesite with my parents, Eva's family, and the others from our kibbutz, I felt like I'd stepped into a twisted fairy tale. Nothing seemed real. My brain seemed to separate itself from my shaking, weeping body as I observed her coffin being lowered into her grave. I longed to talk to Eva about this strange happening. We'd make up some joke about it and then go back to having fun. And then reality would hit me, and once again, I was angry with God.

To this day, 72 years later, whenever I think of Eva, I feel great sadness about losing my precious friend. I get upset that such a kind, courageous girl who'd survived so much suffering and been free for such a short time, died before she'd had a chance to live. And every year, on August 11, tears come to my eyes as I think of Eva, and wish we could have continued to share our lives.

---

22 Polio, or poliomyelitis or infantile paralysis, is a highly contagious, virus that usually begins with chills and fever, and progresses to muscle pains, breathing difficulty, paralysis, and death. Its victims were mostly young children. This terrible disease has been almost 100% eliminated because of the Salk Vaccine invented by Jonas Salk in the early 1950s.

Chapter 15
October 1946-February 1947: *Big Changes*

When I lost Eva, time seemed to stand still. It was as if my world just froze in place. It was strange to see everyone else going about their lives as always, when my life had stopped. Somehow despite my sadness, the weeks flew by, and soon it was time for the 10-day Jewish High Holidays. The first day is *Rosh Hashanah*.[23] Most of us refugees had not celebrated this holiday since before the war, so the days between *Rosh Hashanah* and *Yom Kippur* (the Day of Atonement) would be emotional. Our great happiness that we had survived to celebrate the New Year was filled with great sadness for the tragedy we'd experienced, and for the loved ones who no longer were with us.

Since we were not near a synagogue, the services were held in the huge dining room of our villa kibbutz. Papa was honored and excited because he had been asked to function as both the *rabbi*,[24] leading the spoken parts of the services, and as the *cantor*, leading the singing portions. Papa had a deep, expressive, and melodic voice—both when speaking and singing—so it was always a pleasure to listen to him. I was proud of his many skills, his leadership in the community, and the great respect given to him by so many. During the service, Mama and I

---

23 *Rosh Hashanah* is the first night of the 10-day Jewish High Holy Days celebrating the new year each autumn. The last night is *Yom Kippur,* the "Day of Penitence," when Jews ask forgiveness from those they have hurt or offended.

24 *Rabbi:* A Jewish scholar who teaches students and conducts religious services.

sat close together holding hands, as silent tears blurred our vision and slipped down our cheeks. We were awed by the presence of over 100 brave Jews, who had suffered so grievously, and who now somehow found the strength to face an uncertain future with so much hope. And we ached with the loss of our relatives whose futures were taken from them.

In regard to our own future, after much discussion, Mama and Papa made the heart-wrenching decision to go to the United States instead of Palestine. This decision was based on the fact that we had many loving relatives in the States who would help us. Having lost so many loved-ones, now more than ever, it was important to be with family. As a committed Zionist, whose dream was to settle in Palestine, however, it was difficult for me to accept their decision. Since I had no choice, I silently decided to postpone rather than give up on my dream. I vowed that I'd go to Israel as soon as I had the chance—which I was finally able to do when I was 22.

Our eventual move to the States was currently being arranged by Mama's brothers Henry and Morris, who lived in Brooklyn, New York. This was fortunate for us because the American government required refugees to be "sponsored" by relatives who would guarantee to support them financially. My uncles had signed the necessary documents confirming they would be responsible for us. Mama had to go to various agencies in Rome and Naples to get us the documents we needed in order to leave Italy and enter the USA. We were not alone in this situation—every family was put on a registration list, given a number, and told to be ready when their number came up. This created a lot of pressure because if we weren't ready to go when they called us, our places on the ship would be given to other people.

In the meanwhile, despite our excitement and anxiety, life went on—and we had to live it. Papa and Mama were accomplished, independent people, and they found it difficult to live in a kibbutz for an extended amount of time. It had been okay temporarily, but only until they could establish themselves on their own in the outside world. To do this, Papa would have to earn enough money to support us. Fortunately for us, an unexpected and interesting situation developed that allowed him to do just that.

Many of the Holocaust refugees living in Rome and its suburbs had health problems related to the ordeals they had survived. Their distrust and fear of Italian doctors prevented them from seeking medical care, so their conditions worsened. This growing number of sick people who refused medical care became a threat to the public welfare, and the government did not know what to do about it. So meetings were held, and because my father was such a well-known and respected surgeon, his name came up—along with a creative solution to the problem.

Papa was allowed operating privileges at Rome's largest hospital—without having an Italian medical license. He was given everything he needed, and paid by the Italian government, as long as he provided care only for Jewish refugees. Papa quickly became busy, sometimes performing three surgeries a day. Now that he had a steady job with a steady income, he decided it was time to leave the kibbutz.

Papa found us a room to rent in an apartment building on Via de La Giuliana, not far from his hospital in Rome. Everyone was sad to see us go, and before we moved, the kibbutzniks gave us a big farewell party. Many of the residents got up to pay their respects to my father, and to show their love for Mama and me.

Mama, Papa, and I are honored at kibbutz farewell party in Monte Mario, Italy: 1947

The members of the Monte Mario kibbutz give us a farewell party. Italy: 1947

Many had either known or heard about Papa's courageous and legendary actions with the partisans, the incredible hospital he built and ran in the forest, and his current skill as a surgeon for the Jewish community in Rome. Everywhere we went, Dr. Chaim Miasnik was a hero to so many people. And while I was thrilled to hear others praise Papa's actions, I also knew that they would miss him terribly. I felt a little guilty that we were leaving these wonderful people to follow our own dream of living on our own.

Mama, Papa, and I moved into one room in a small apartment belonging to Signorina Mery, and her young niece, Helena. Mery was a lively and warm-hearted woman, who swept us up into her heart as if we were her own long-lost relatives. She went out of her way to teach us how to live in Rome, making sure we knew all about the best Italian food, including the traditional bean soup called pasta *fagiole*, which I still love to this day. She patiently taught us important Italian words and phrases, and took Helena and me on field trips, showing us the highlights of Rome, including the Vatican, where the Pope lived, and the famous Trevi Fountains— *Fontana di Trevi.*[25] Mery became a trusted and beloved friend to us. And Helena became the younger sister I'd never had— except that instead of me watching out for her, she watched out for me.

Helena was two years younger than me, but she was smart, and knew much more than I did about being a kid in Rome. And unlike me, she had already been to school for five years. I really depended on her when Mama enrolled me in the elementary school down the street. Even though I wore a uniform and looked like the other kids, it was clear that I was different. First of all, the only Italian words I could speak were what I'd learned on my own in the streets—so I probably sounded rude.

Furthermore, other than what I'd learned from their comic books, I didn't know anything about Italian culture. I didn't understand what the other kids were talking about. I definitely didn't understand when they made fun of me, which seemed to be one of their favorite activities. Worst of all, I was put in the fourth grade even though I'd never finished first through third grades. Helena protected me as much as she could, and I felt bad when it caused the others to pick on her, as well.

I'd always been intensely curious and loved to learn, so I'd expected to do well in school, and had been excited about going. I was, therefore, totally stunned by my failure to succeed. And each day brought more frustration, anxiety, and self-doubt. Since I couldn't read the Italian text books, or communicate with the teachers, I never had a chance to succeed. And it seemed as if I couldn't do

25 *The Trevi Fountain,* located in the Trevi district in Rome, Italy, was designed by Nicola Salvii, is one of the most famous fountains in the world.

anything right. I had gone from being an active, intelligent, multi-lingual 11-year old who spoke Yiddish, Polish, Russian, and Romanian, to being a depressed, stressed-out, utter failure. It was a sickening shock to me, and I longed for my lost friend, Eva, and the comfort she would have brought me. My parents were surprised and disappointed that I was failing, so they took me out of school and hired a tutor for me, but I still made little progress. I hated letting my parents down, but I also felt that they were letting me down by not understanding that I couldn't make progress if I didn't understand what I was reading or hearing.

Thankfully, after three months, I was rescued from this madness. In January 1947, my parents received an official notification from the American Embassy in Naples: we had been granted visas[26] to go to the United States. I was almost delirious with joy—and it wasn't entirely because I'd be getting away from my hated Italian school! I'd seen fabulous movies and heard about the wonders of America ever since we'd been liberated. It was the land of freedom and opportunity, where everyone was happy, and loving families lived in their own homes and had adorable pet dogs. I felt as if were wriggling out of a tight scratchy, pain-filled cocoon, and I was more than ready to fly. My life was about to begin—finally!

We had to be ready to leave as soon as our ship was available—if we weren't ready, our spots would be given to other refugees. One afternoon, when I was home alone, the phone rang. When I answered it, a crisp, official sounding voice told me that our ship was ready to board in Naples. Despite my shaking hand, I managed to write down the details so that I'd be able to give my parents the correct information. Then, unable to contain my joy, I danced around the house, grinning from ear to ear! When my parents walked through the door, I threw myself at them, breathlessly telling them the good news. Then the three of us hugged, while laughing and crying tears of joy.

The next day, we hired a car to take us to the shipyard in Naples. Signorina Mery went with us, and cried the whole way. Clutching her damp hankie and weeping, she hugged each of us to her heart, told us she loved us, wished us well, and made us promise to write to her as soon as we arrived in New York. While we felt sad at leaving Signora Mery and Helena, our spirits soared as we looked up at the massive ship looming above us. This was the ship that would be taking us to our new lives of freedom and comfort in America—*di goldene medine* (the land of gold). We could barely contain our excitement! In the back of my mind, however, was some concern, because the *SS Marine Falcon* was old and ugly. It looked like a prison instead of a ship that would be taking us to the land of our dreams.

26   A visa is a government document that allows a person to legally enter a foreign country.

SS *Marine Falcon* (Illustration by Angel L. Luna)

My gloomy feeling intensified as we climbed aboard. Much to our sad surprise, we quickly learned that we would not be crossing the ocean in a cozy private room. I wouldn't be gazing at the endless ocean through a cute round porthole. Instead, we women and children—mostly Italians—were directed to large, windowless, and plain cabins, that were filled wall-to-wall with cots. Mama and I would be sharing one of these cabins with around 150 other females of all ages.

Men and boys were sent to similar communal cabins. This was definitely not my idea of how we should travel. There was no privacy, and when the sea was rough, the cots and our belongings would slide across the floor and bump into each other. It felt like a floating displaced persons' camp—one which smelled awful because the residents were often violently seasick and throwing-up. Making the situation worse was that the communal lavatory was down the hall, and sick people couldn't always get there in time. I was not surprised at all when I learned that the tired, old, steamship, *SS Marine Falcon* had not been designed as a passenger ship. It had been transporting soldiers and equipment and other cargo for decades. International relief agencies had joined together and taken it over to transport refugees to America. It had only a couple voyages left before it would be sent to the scrap heap.

Mama and I found our cots, looked around the depressing cabin, then looked at each other in silence. We were both thinking the same thing: We've lived in far worse conditions, so let's make the best of it. We each had one suitcase, which we'd put down next to our cots, and then we met Papa back on the crowded deck to wave goodbye to Italy, to Europe, and to the past. As the ship backed away into the open waters of the Bay of Naples, our eyes clouded over, and the salty ocean spray mixed with our tears. Yes, we were more than ready to leave Europe, and eager to start a new life in a place called Brooklyn, in a free nation somewhere beyond the horizon. And yes, we were free—free to live, and free to partake of life's bounties and blessings. But we would never be free of the haunting ache of our lost loved ones. So we wept for all those millions of Jews who had perished, including Aunt Ala, Uncle Tadek, my father's mother, Chana Liba, my mother's parents, and so many other relatives and close friends. And I also wept for Eva, who managed to survive the Nazis, but who never had a chance for a life.

Chapter 16

February 1947: *Greenhorns in the Golden Land*

Eventually, my tears dried, and as the ship sailed slowly past the huge Rock of Gibraltar into the open waters of the Atlantic Ocean, I felt as if itchy, shreds of my painful past were peeling off of me like slivers of sunburned skin. And all too soon, I would learn that the emerging soft skin would be unprotected. As I stared out at the endless blue water, and day-dreamed about what life would be like in America, I couldn't have forseen that life in America would be different from Hollywood movies. And that it would bring me a new kind of pain.

I'd seen movies of American families living in large houses, surrounded by colorful gardens. There would also be fruit trees from which I would eat my fill. I could see myself laughing and playing in the big grassy yard with my happy, healthy, American friends. Suddenly, the faces of these friends morphed into the faces of my beloved lost friends. I saw wide-eyed, dirty, bleeding, Tuska, wearing rags as she stood alone in the door of our empty house after the Lida Massacre. I saw Halinka, my little friend in Szczuczyn, who'd been rescued by a Christian family when she ran from the train that deported her parents. I saw happy, energetic Eva—who'd had so much to live for—lose her fight with polio. How I wish I could have brought them with me to the States. How I wish now, at age 84, they could somehow know that I still carry them in my heart.

Angry storm clouds rolled in as I stared at the disappearing skyline of Europe, and my hopes for a bright future in American darkened along with sky. Our immediate future definitely was not looking bright and sunny. Just as we entered the Atlantic Ocean, its blue water turned black and a major storm erupted—tossing our huge ship around like a small, helpless, plastic bathtub toy. Mama, Papa, and I raced to our cabins in order to avoid getting drenched—or worse, being washed overboard.

In the cabins, closely packed cots rolled around as if they were balls in a pinball machine, banging into each other, while we stumbled and tried to avoid falling on other people. As women and girls fell, their shrieks filled the air. Also filling the air were the sounds—and smells—of these women throwing up as they tried—and failed—to get to the bathrooms in time. The storm lasted for days, and during that time, Mama and I were unable to eat. It was worse for her, and as she got weaker and weaker, terrifying memories of her sickness in the forest camp flooded through me. Fortunately, we both recovered as soon as the storm blew over.

Once I was able to eat again, I got a big surprise: grapefruit! My taste buds thrilled at its indescribable sweet tartness. Another wonderful surprise was the kindness of the American crew members who made a point of speaking slowly in order to help us understand English. Since I had a good ear, and already spoke five languages, it was easy for me to pick up words and phrases. I loved it when they told us about American food, American movies, and sang American songs. I was surprised that they knew about Brooklyn! One bad surprise was when I learned a new word that at first made me sad—and then made me angry. The word was "greenhorn," and it was an insult that Americans used to describe refugees. Greenhorns were considered dirty, ignorant, and inferior, and they were handy topics for degrading jokes. It was humiliating to think that others would view me as a greenhorn.

When the weather allowed, Mama, Papa, and I would sit outside on the deck, watching rays of sun play on the endless water. We would sing the precious Yiddish songs that had been so important to our lives. In a way, singing these songs brought us comfort and strength to face what lay ahead. Papa had told us that since Americans hadn't experienced the horrific Third Reich, that they wouldn't believe what we had gone through. They might even think we were lying. For sure, they would not understand what had happened to us. I was worried that I would be seen as a weird outsider, and never find a true friend. Despite these worries, however, my parents and I looked forward to finally having a home—whatever "home" meant.

In the misty gray dawn light on February 23, 1947, we approached a huge landmass on the horizon. The decks of ship became crowded with passengers rushing to see the great United States come into view. Everyone seemed to be hypnotized by the sight of the Stature of Liberty, who welcomed us into New York harbor. Even though I didn't know what the Statue of Liberty represented, I was also overwhelmed. My mother's eyes lit up, and she started waving and jumping up and down when she somehow spotted her brother Henry in the crowd below. With tears in her eyes she pointed with her finger, "Chaim, Mirele, look over there. It is Henry. Wave!" All I could see were hundreds of smiling people awaiting the other passengers, but I was relieved and delighted to know that we would soon be greeted by our own loving relatives. After eight harrowing years, we were no longer alone.

When our ship docked, there was complete chaos. We were part of an impatient, nervous, and excited crowd. Everywhere I looked, people were jostling each other, and trying to hang on to their suitcases and small children, while moving toward the ship's exit. It was next to impossible to communicate effectively, and tempers flared. We got into the wrong lines several times, and it took hours for us to get off the ship and then through customs.[27] Unlike many others, we didn't have to have a medical exam or answer a lot of questions. To our relief, the customs officers just looked through our suitcases and purses, and waved us on.

Having finished the requirements of Customs, we were free to go breathe the free air of America. We rushed through the exit and into our new lives. We were joyfully swooped up by my three uncles: Uncle Henry, Morris and Bernie (my father's brother), and my adult cousin Miriam, into a laughing, crying, group hug. I was especially happy to see Miriam, because I actually remembered her from my early childhood in Warsaw. Deep and overpowering emotions welled-up from our hearts as our arms reached for and held onto each other. After eight hideous years, my parents and I were safe with our own loving relatives.

At the same time, however, I had emotions that my parents would never share or understand. All these tearful people grasping me close and covering me with kisses were strangers to me. Yes, I recognized their faces from photographs, and had heard stories about them, but I didn't have any real-life connection with them. In fact, it was overwhelming to be the center of their attention. Amidst the hugs, kisses, teary eyes, endless comments about how tall I'd grown, and questions about how I was doing . . . it felt as if I were being smothered by kindness. I didn't know what to say to them, and since I was afraid I'd say the wrong thing, I kept quiet. Then they all worried about why I was so quiet, and they tried to get me to talk. Which of course, only made me retreat further back into my shell.

---

27 Customs is a section of a government building where officials determine if incoming passengers can be admitted to the country.

They couldn't hear the silent shrieks of pain and loss that were trapped inside their scrawny, sad-eyed eleven-year old relative. I knew they were my family and they loved me, so I felt guilty that I couldn't respond to them. But the only "family" I remembered were my Aunt Ala and my grandparents. And I cried for their absence as much as I cried in relief at being in America. I also cried as I realized that in my beautiful new life of freedom, I would never be free of the past.

Finally able to untangle from our hugs, we divided into groups and squeezed into two taxis to that strange, exotic place I'd heard of: Brooklyn! The rest of the world seemed to disappear as I gazed unblinkingly out the window, waiting to see the glittering streets that I'd heard were paved in gold. Unfortunately, the streets were gray, dingy, and littered with garbage. They reminded me of the slums in Rome. Instead of the grand apartment buildings I'd expected, all I saw were blocks and blocks of tightly-packed, old, decrepit buildings called *tenements,* and crowds of raggedy poor people in the streets. My dreams of living in the "land of plenty" had already begun to dissolve.

During our cab ride to Brooklyn, Mama and Uncle Morris spoke mostly in Yiddish and Polish, but even though I could understand them, I remained silent, adrift in my own world. Ironically, Uncle Morris' kind efforts to cheer me up had the exact opposite effect. He brought up the topic of going to school. This definitely was not a topic that would calm my fears or cheer me up. I now understand that he thought I'd be excited to attend an American school, but at that moment, I instantly disliked him for further spoiling my arrival in America. He was a kind, loving man who wouldn't have known that I had only bad memories of going to school. In fact, the very thought of going to yet another school where I didn't know anyone and didn't speak or read their language, made me sick to my stomach. All I could envision were failure and humiliation. So I didn't answer him. I'm sure he thought there was something very wrong with me. And in a way, there was.

We arrived after dark at the Brooklyn apartment building where both of Mama's brothers lived. Many relatives and friends had crowded in Uncle Henry and Aunt Ethel's small apartment to greet us. These included Uncle Morris and his wife, Lillian, their children Benjy, Michael, and Abraham. Papa's brother Bernie, his wife Aunt Anna, and their daughters Lorraine and Marsha, had travelled all the way from Pennsylvania to be part of this joyous reunion. I was relieved to recognize some of them from photographs they'd sent to us in Italy.

We all sat around the table trying to communicate in Polish or in Yiddish—usually a mixture of both. Having had years of practice at being silent, I sat quietly next to my mother. She and Papa were the center of attention as they described our experiences during the war. With heavy hearts, they spoke of Ala,

Tadek, and my grandparents who had perished. When the faces around the table began to crumble in pain, Papa lightened the conversation, by describing our lives in the partisans. To our relatives, our time in the forest must have sounded like a thrilling adventure story.

As all eyes locked on Papa, my eyes caught sight of—and locked on—a fruit bowl. It contained ripe, yellow bananas. And I desperately wanted one. I had only eaten one banana in my entire life, and its unusual appearance and sweet taste seemed almost magical to me. Since Mama had strictly warned me to watch my manners, and for sure not to grab anything on the table, I was afraid to ask for one. Finally, unable to resist the urge any longer, I shocked everyone by finally talking. In a room suddenly bursting with silence, I softly asked in Yiddish if I could please have a banana. My request was instantly fulfilled, and I must have looked like a crazed little monkey as I devoured it with gusto. I immediately asked for a second . . . and then a third. My relatives probably would have given me bananas forever, just to hear me talk! To this day, a banana is right up there with grapefruit in symbolizing the abundance of delicious food in America.

The family had decided that we would stay at Uncle Henry and Aunt Ethel's small two-bedroom apartment until we were able to live on our own. This meant that my cousins, Michael and Benjy, had to share their parents' bedroom. Since Mama, Papa, and I had lived in actual holes in the snow-covered ground, we didn't mind crowding together. Mama and Papa shared a bed, and I slept on a cot. We were happy just to be warm, safe, and not hungry. It must have been difficult, however, for my Aunt, Uncle and cousins to be cooped up in one bedroom. We never heard any complaints from them—clearly, their love for us was more important than their own privacy and comfort. On our first night in America, we breathed easily as we finally slept in freedom and safety—with full stomachs.

Our life in America began bright and early the next morning with our first real American breakfast. In addition to toast with butter and jam, it included cold cereal and—much to my delight—bananas! I loved

This was the first photo taken in the States. We are on the boardwalk across the street from Uncle Henry's apartment near Sheepshead Bay, New York: 1947

the orange juice and was flabbergasted at all the milk the children drank. It was as if they had an unlimited supply of everything. For several days, right after breakfast, we were visited by a stream of family members and friends who were eager to meet us. In the weeks that followed, my cousins and I strolled through the streets along Sheepshead Bay. It reminded me of the beautiful Lido of Venice, and I loved looking at the boats. We also window-shopped, and I was stunned by the endless variety of stores and products. Our favorite destination on these walks was my uncles' pharmacy which was located just inside the subway station. It had an ice cream soda fountain where we could enjoy our favorite treats.

These walks helped me to learn my way around and adjust to my new world. My fears faded a bit and I felt more confident, because I was protected by my

cousins. Michael and Benjy enjoyed pointing out interesting buildings, and were always eager to help me learn English. I'd begun to pick up some English words and phrases on my own, so I was able to understand snatches of conversations I heard out on the streets. After days of window-shopping, I was finally able to go into one of the stores! Uncle Morris and Aunt Lillian took me shopping for real American clothes. I was delighted that they bought me brand new blue jeans! Now I would look like a real American teenager!

Despite the progress I was making, however, I still felt the pain of great loneliness—the pain of not belonging anywhere. It was so hard to be in the midst of crowds of people and not understand what they are saying—or thinking. I longed to be surrounded by a language I could understand! Fortunately, my Uncle's radio picked up an Italian station, and I could happily listen to it for hours. Of all the shows, the operas were my favorites. I felt a happy glow of contentment as I

I was so proud of my first pair of American blue jeans and their fancy pockets! Brooklyn: 1947

remembered the brilliant opera singers on the streets of Rome. Unfortunately, my Aunt Ethel became annoyed with me for being glued to the Italian station. She'd turn it off, telling me, "It's time for you to be learning English, forget the Italian, you won't need it." I know now, that she was concerned about my future, but I still needed my few comforts from the past. It hurt that she did not understand my need to hear something that was familiar.

Aunt Ethel was not the only person who meant well but was insensitive to my feelings. Since I wasn't able to protect myself, my pain often turned to anger. This anger caused me to distance myself even further from the people who thought they were helping me, and so I ended up being even more lonely. I would get especially upset by thoughtless remarks such as, "How lucky you are to have gone through the war as a child instead of as an adult, soon you won't remember any of it. Your parents were the unlucky ones." And, "You were too young to know what was really happening—only an adult could fully understand what was going on during the war."

How could these people who had never experienced Nazi terror possibly think they could judge me? They did not have the right to decide what I should feel or not feel. It was as if they were erasing my hugely profound, true experiences, and re-drawing my life, making it smaller to fit their own shallow need to think they were helping me. Rather than make the effort to understand what I was going through, it was easier for them to believe there was something wrong with me: "She's too shy. She's too quiet. She only speaks Polish and Yiddish. She doesn't make an effort to fit in. She is not grateful for all we do for her."

They could not possibly understand my reality or ever truly help me because they looked at me through eyes that were incapable of seeing. While they knew the fact that our relatives had died, they didn't know the *emotion* of it. They didn't have the heart-pounding memories of it. And they could never understand what it meant to have *survived*—to be one of the Holocaust's *living victims*.

How shocked they would all have been if they had known that their actions made me feel as if I didn't really belong in America. As if I didn't belong in my own family. And just when I thought they couldn't hurt me anymore, they came up with yet another supposedly helpful opinion that just added further heat to the fire of my misery: "It will be easy for you to learn a new language and adjust to a new lifestyle, Mirka. You are young enough to forget the past. Wait till you go to school."

Learn a new language? How many languages did *they* know? I knew five before I was ten years old. Adjust to a new lifestyle? I'd done nothing but adjust to new lifestyles—constantly. Being a silent, terrified, secret "niece" at the farmhouse, returning to the ghost-filled Lida ghetto after the massacre, living in dank, dark holes under snow, hiding in rotted tree trunks, living under brutal Soviet control, sleeping on a hard chair in an empty store in Lublin on Passover, being grateful to be uncomfortable in refugee camp tents, following rules in military compounds, feeling at home with other kibbutzim, sharing rented rooms in strangers' apartments . . . I was the queen of adjusting to different lifestyles.

Forget about my past?

Never.

Chapter 17

March 1947-January 1949: *School Daze*

I was, in fact, learning to understand English, but I didn't think I'd ever really need it so I avoided speaking it. What I'd seen of Americans was definitely not positive, and I had no desire to interact with them. Why would I even want to fit in with them? They seemed silly, shallow, spoiled—and boring. They had nothing interesting to say because their lives had been too easy. And the thought of having to go to an American school terrified me. Sadly, my terrified thoughts were soon followed by even more terrifying action.

On a Friday morning, two weeks after we'd arrived in America, Mama told me to wear something nice because she and Uncle Henry were taking me to register for school. We walked two blocks to PS 225, and found our way to the principal's office. Uncle Henry carried on the conversation with the principal in English, and translated into Polish for Mama. It was hard for me to follow the quick translations, and the constant, robotic, smile of the principal irritated me, so I just tuned the whole thing out.

Despite Mama and Uncle Henry's cheerful assurances that I would love going to an American school, and making new friends, I knew from my experience in Rome that it was going to be awful. What was also awful was that I had reached a point in my life where I realized that the adults who were in charge of me had no idea of what my actual reality was like. I felt completely disconnected and even more alone than before. It was weird.

Starting school in March meant that I had three months before summer vacation. For some reason, my parents fully expected me to pass the entire fifth grade in three months, without having completed the first six months—without having completed first through fourth grades—without being able to speak, read, or understand English. How could such a thing be possible? I realized that not only did my parents not understand me—I did not understand them. Where did our one-for-all and all-for-one team spirit go? I was used to being part of a threesome that depended on each other to survive. A team that was totally interconnected and supportive. A team where we all had the same goals. Suddenly, everything had shifted, and I was not only on my own, but it felt as if Mama and Papa's goals were the opposite of mine.

When my birthday arrived on March 10, there was a birthday cake, and I received some new clothes, but all I felt was misery. This definitely was not what I'd expected to be feeling on my 12th birthday. And then, a few days later, on a windy, cold Monday morning, things got even worse. Mama woke me up early, gave me breakfast, and then along with Benjy, and Michael, walked me to school. It felt as if they were taking me to prison.

The only thing I was grateful for was that my cousins went to the same school. Even though we didn't speak the same language, they were kind, and I knew they would do their best to watch out for me. Mama gave me a hug in the schoolyard, and then the boys helped me find my room. The teacher smiled, and probably introduced herself, but I didn't know what she was saying. She pointed to my desk and gave me my school books. Looking down at the floor, I walked stiffly to my seat and began a routine that would last for several weeks. I sat alone in shame and silence. None of the kids spoke to me and I could tell by their looks, whispers, and giggles they thought I was weird. Even now I wonder why it was so hard for them to understand that I had come from a different continent and spoke several different languages. I just didn't speak theirs.

Some of the Jewish teachers understood my situation and offered to help me after school. Even after I'd learned enough English to realize they were being kind, my fear of school prevented me from staying even one more minute there than I had to—even for help. When each day ended, I just had to escape as soon as possible. I'd spent my whole life locking my fears up in some dark corner of my soul, and now, it was as if that door had burst open. My new fears just added to those that were already there, making it impossible to close the door. My fear of the other students, my fear of the teachers, my fear of failure, of disappointing my parents, of looking weird, talking weird—my fear of life itself—all these fears overwhelmed me. So as usual, I withdrew further into my own silent world. It was my only safe haven.

Mama and Papa didn't need a safe haven. They were busy moving on with their lives—making up for the years they'd lost. Papa was taking classes and studying night and day for the tests he had to take in order to become a licensed physician in America. His biggest challenge was learning enough English to understand and respond to the questions on the tests. Mama began working afternoons behind the lunch counter in my uncles' pharmacy. This was a real treat for me because she was in charge of the ice cream and sodas. Mama earned 25 dollars per week, and within a few weeks, we were able to move out of Uncle Henry's apartment. Our next home was a small furnished room in a private home of a single middle-aged man on Avenue Y in an area of Brooklyn called Sheepshead Bay. Our room had two beds, and we were allowed to use the kitchen. Mama was happy because it was close to the pharmacy, so she wouldn't have such a long walk every day. Unfortunately for me, our new home was not in the PS 225 school district. Or even near it. In order not to disrupt my school semester, my parents decided I should continue going to PS 225, even though it was a really long daily walk. Further adding to my frustration was that since everyone in our neighborhood attended the nearby school, I had to make that long walk to and from school by myself every day. It's funny how this walk seemed so difficult when just a few years before, I'd walked much longer distances in the forest—in all kinds of weather, and in constant danger.

While my weekdays were miserable, everything changed on Saturday afternoons. This was when Mama and I continued our tradition from Rome of going to the movies. We'd buy popcorn and Cokes, find seats that weren't obstructed by tall people wearing hats, and settle back for a trip into another world. I especially loved action-packed war movies. I liked seeing Germans getting beaten in battles with the Allied armies. I also loved movies about children who'd had to overcome monumental obstacles. My favorite was *The Search*. It was released in 1948, and tells the story of a young Auschwitz survivor and his mother who had been separated from each other. After the war, they searched for each other across the ruins of post-World War II Germany. I could relate to these events because they were so similar to my own experiences. Even today, when I watch it and see what that little boy went through, I get tears in my eyes.

After a few weeks, much to my surprise, I actually began to make some progress in school. I was able to do well in simple arithmetic because numbers, unlike words, are the same in every language. And as I learned more English, I did well in geography, especially European geography. I had, after all, traveled through most of Europe after the war. Much to my even bigger surprise, my first report card was not bad—but since it also was not good, my parents were disappointed in me. As a result, I became depressed that I hadn't done better. It seemed that no matter how much progress I made, no matter how many obstacles I overcame, I still wasn't living up to their expectations.

Speaking of not living up to expectations, America had definitely not lived up to mine. My life in Italy had been much better. Furthermore, I was frustrated that we had not gone to Israel, where I would be together with other child survivors, most of whom spoke Polish and Yiddish. And since I wouldn't have a language problem, I would also be able to succeed in an Israeli school, which would please my parents. Sadly, I was not in Israel, so I was really looking forward to summer, and a break from school as well as from my daily frustrations. I planned to hang out alone in my room and listen to my radio. I would go for walks by myself, and read a few books. Best of all, I wouldn't have to deal with other people—especially Americans. I'd given a lot of thought to my plans for summer, and the relief it would bring me. My parents, however, already had plans for my summer. And they were totally different from mine.

Papa's two brothers, Bernie and Charlie, who lived in Pennsylvania, owned a butcher shop. They worked hard, were successful, and earned enough money to rent a cottage on a peaceful lake, where their wives and children spent the summers. Bernie's daughters, Marsha and Lorraine were close to my age. It was decided that I should spend my first American summer at the cottage with my relatives. Mama told me that being free to run around with my cousins in the cool, clean, fresh air would be healthier for me than being cooped up and alone in a hot, humid Brooklyn room. An added benefit was that I would be able to improve my English and learn more about American customs from the girls. Of course, I hated the idea at first. I *wanted* to be cooped up alone in a hot, humid room in Brooklyn. I didn't really know my cousins, and since they were *American,* I figured they would be mean to me, and I'd be treated as an outsider. I'd already had so much bad luck, that being stranded so far from my parents—even if they didn't understand me—seemed like it could only bring more bad luck.

Fortunately, my luck was about to change.

My cousins' summer cottage was a charming old wooden house facing beautiful lake. When I first saw it, I breathed a huge sigh of relief. I'd never spent time at a lake, and seeing its beauty gave me hope that the summer would not be a total disaster. The cottage was spacious, and even though I shared a room with my cousins, there were plenty of places I could go when I needed my privacy. We spent many lazy days at the lake, and I even learned to swim that summer. Lorraine was two years older, and taller, and more mature than I was. She had started hanging out with boys. I felt repulsed by the American boys I met in New York. Their only talent was talking about the batting averages of base-ball players. My cousins often teased me because of the way I pronounced some English letters. "Love," came out as "wuv," because in Polish "L" is pronounced as "W." But even though the jokes were on me, it was good to laugh because, one, I understood the jokes, and two, we laughed together. I was actually having fun, and this allowed me to forget the realities of life in Brooklyn. I even forgot that I was a bit mad at Mama for sending me off to the cottage. Much to my surprise, I missed having her around.

My cousins did a good job of "Americanizing" me, and so when I returned home at the end of summer 1947, I understood Americans better. And because of this, I was much more comfortable being around them. My growing confidence even allowed me to feel more comfortable with myself, because I wasn't always afraid that I'd do or say the wrong thing. Mama had managed to save enough money for us to move again. This time it would be to our own apartment on Neptune Avenue, near Brighton Beach. This was more space than we'd had to ourselves since our Warsaw apartment before the war. I was excited when my mother bought me a desk for my room. Maybe it would be a good omen for my schoolwork. And so, in a tiny way, much to my own big surprise, I looked forward to going to a new school in the fall—especially since this school was within close walking distance.

On my first day at PS 100, I was happily surprised that I had been assigned to the 7th grade. So even though I hadn't attended first through fourth grade, and even though I'd attended only the last three months of 5th grade, and even though I was still learning English, I'd somehow managed to skip 6th grade. I was nervous that I wouldn't be able to keep up with the other kids, but I was relieved to no longer be so much older than my classmates. Also, my English improved, so I began to understand more of my schoolwork. Spelling, grammar, and history were still difficult, but I was doing well in math, science, geography and music. I even became friends with two American Jewish girls who lived nearby. And as the semester progressed with no catastrophes, I grew less depressed and anxious.

And I wasn't the only one making progress. Papa's endless studying finally paid off, and he passed the medical board licensing tests. He was now qualified to practice medicine in the state of New York. This was a huge accomplishment and we were so proud of him! He immediately began a short internship at a hospital in Brooklyn, and once again he had interesting stories of his days' events. One in particular happened soon after he began working there helped to establish Papa's reputation for excellence. He had recognized that one of the patients had a case of typhoid fever. He immediately reported it to the man's doctor but was told that it couldn't possibly be typhoid, so he should mind his own business, and stay away from the patient.

Of course this rude response didn't stop Papa. He'd seen hundreds of cases of typhoid, and definitely knew its symptoms. Since he knew how contagious it was, and how deadly it could be, he reported the case to the Board of Health. A few weeks later, the hospital and the Board of Health officially thanked my father for his astute diagnosis. He had prevented a possible hospital—and city-wide—epidemic. Once again, Mama and I were so proud of this man who had endured so much, worked so hard, and helped so many. This was a profound achievement for Papa—and for Mama and for me.

For the first time since 1939, we were safe, we were free, and at last, we were on our way to becoming Americans.

My 8th grade graduation,
Brooklyn, NY: January 1949

Chapter 18
January 1949: *A Victory for Miriam!*

An important part of becoming Americans was changing our foreign-sounding last name to something easier to remember. We also needed something that would be more pleasing to the American ear than Miasnik. Since Papa's brothers had already changed their last name to Mason, Mama and Papa did the same, and we became Betty, Henry, and Miriam Mason.

As always, my parents worked hard and planned for the next stage of our lives. By mid-1948, since they could now afford to stop renting, they started searching for a house to buy. Their plan was to find a two-story house that would allow Papa to use the ground floor for his medical office. They also hoped it would be in a Jewish neighborhood. They found exactly what they wanted in Brighton Beach. An added bonus was that it was close to my uncles. And happily for me, I would be able to remain at my present school. Mama would stop working at the pharmacy, in order to run Papa's office. The day we moved into our new home, Papa hung his "shingle" (a sign indicating that this was the location of Dr. Mason's office) from a pole in the garden outside our front door. Papa's reputation grew and eventually, he was invited to join the staffs of two hospitals, where he performed surgery.

Papa's medical practice grew quickly. He was especially beloved by the Jewish community, where he was considered to be a hero. They revered him not only because of his work with the partisans, but because of his kindness to his current patients, most of whom were immigrants, and many of whom were Holocaust survivors. In addition to providing quality and compassionate medical care,

Papa's office "shingle"

Papa helped many people financially. Without saying a word, he would slip a couple of dollars into the pocket of a needy patient. He even hid special small jars throughout his office, and at the end of each day, he'd empty his pockets and put the change in the jars. This way he always had cash on hand in case a patient needed it. Mama and I were so proud of his quiet generosity that we never let him know we knew about the jars.

Our lives took on a sense of normal routine. And while some people might find this boring, for us it was a welcome relief. It was comfortable to have a secure place to live, a steady income, a school where I was able to achieve, along with dear family and friends. We enjoyed being respected and loved members of the Jewish community. And it was wonderful seeing Mama bloom. I'd never known her when her family's life wasn't in danger, so this was a whole new Mama for me.

There was a downside to my parents' new lives. They were so busy, that I often felt alone and abandoned. In addition to her activities with the Jewish community, Mama worked hard in Papa's office. Papa devoted himself to his patients, so we rarely saw him. I was saddened that we seemed to have lost the sense of closeness we'd had during the war, when we were united against our enemies. There was a benefit to this separation, however, because it coincided with my natural teenage instinct to become independent.

As I became more fluent in English, it was easier for me to interact with my classmates. And I finally made a friend, a sweet girl named Charlotte, who lived across the street.

We walked to school together, and were in some of the same classes. After school and on weekends, we went to the movies and hung out at the beach. While we hadn't started dating yet, a highlight of our activities was meeting and talking with boys. Since I was busy becoming an American, I didn't mention my childhood experiences in Europe.

My days continued to bring progress, comfort, and independence. There were even some days that I wasn't consciously haunted by my past—some days when a familiar-looking face didn't make my heart race with thoughts of lost loved ones. There were even nights that my dreams were not filled with Nazis, terror, and death. And even though I still didn't completely fit in to my new life in America, I definitely was making progress, and I felt as if I were finally leaving my troubled past behind.

In January 1949, as graduation drew near, I was surprised and proud to learn I would be given a special PTA (Parent-Teacher Association) award. This was given to the student who had made the most progress in learning. Even though I hadn't realized it, my teachers had been paying attention to my determination to achieve—and they were proud of my accomplishments. I was happy to be able to bring this good news to my parents, and to finally make them proud of me.

On the afternoon of graduation, as I walked across the stage toward the smiling Mr. Sammet, I felt a little smile of my own break through my usually worried-looking face. And as my hand broke through the mist of the past to grasp my diploma, a strange and exhilarating new feeling flooded my senses.

It was the thrill of victory.

EPILOGUE

Throughout the 80 years from the day that the Germans attacked Warsaw Poland, turning the life of an innocent four year-old girl upside down, until today, safe in her beautiful Ann Arbor, Michigan home, Miriam Miasnik Brysk has confronted and won more than her share of battles. That she has been victorious in spite of often impossible odds, is a tribute to her intellect, bravery, curiosity, loving heart, and self-discipline. At the age of 84 her victories not only continue, but they continue to touch the hearts of all who know and gain inspiration from her life.

After her eighth-grade graduation, Miriam went on to high school, where she finally began to feel comfortable enough with herself to start making friends. She was delighted to be invited to join a girls' social club. She also actively pursued her interest in Zionism, and found the comfort and deep friendships she'd always longed for when she joined *Habonim,* a Zionist youth group. In 1952, five years after coming to the United States, she graduated from high school, and began studying to become a scientist at New York University. In one of her life's most important victories, she became an American citizen. And while the future would bring her more battles—there would also be more victories.

In addition to becoming an American legally in 1952, Miriam became an American emotionally. She felt profound gratitude to the country that took her family in, and gave them the freedom not only to dream—but to make their dreams come true. One of her dreams was to pursue a career in science, which she did with great dedication. Miriam ultimately earned a Ph.D in Biological Sciences from Columbia University in New York City, and became a highly respected scientist and medical school professor, teaching in three different departments at the University of Texas.

In 1953, Miriam went on a "blind date" with Henry Brysk, a brilliant physicist, who was also a Holocaust survivor, from Paris, France. They fell

Miriam and Henry on honeymoon
The Poconos, Pennsylvania: 1955

in love, married in 1955, and built a wonderful life together which includes their loving and accomplished daughters, Dr. Judy Brysk, MD, and Dr. Havi Brysk Mandell, Ph.D, artist and therapist. Adding to their joy are their beautiful grandchildren: Ben, Josh, Hannah, David and Sarah, and most recently, their precious great-grandson, Elian. When Miriam looks at her beloved family, she also sees images of the family she lost during the Holocaust. Her heart understands all too well, that if her parents had made a different decision on that fateful night in the Lida ghetto, none of them would have been born. Miriam and Henry celebrated their 64th wedding anniversary in June 2019, and as they gazed into each other's eyes, and they felt blessed that they had the vision to go on that blind date in 1953!

Miriam and Henry's wedding
New York City: 1955

Miriam and Henry
Ann Arbor, Michigan: 2017

In 2000, at age 65, Miriam retired from her long and acclaimed career as a scientist. In the fall of 2002, Miriam and Henry traveled to Eastern Europe with a Jewish tour group led by University of Michigan Holocaust Scholar, Dr. Zvi Gittelman. When the group arrived at Treblinka, where Miriam's family, along with 250,000 other Jews from the Warsaw ghetto were murdered, overwhelming waves of emotion flooded through her. Miriam walked off by herself to say the Mourners' Kaddish (Jewish prayer for the dead), and then, with tears streaming down her face, she softly sang the song, "Treblinka." This moment marked a profound change in Miriam's life, and inspired her to make a pact with God to dedicate her remaining years to Holocaust remembrance.

Upon returning home, Miriam decided to use art as a medium for honoring the victims of the Holocaust, and she began a new career as a digital artist. Her three highly acclaimed Holocaust art exhibits have been displayed in 38 venues, including museums, galleries, and private collections. Three of her works are in the permanent collection of Yad Vashem - The World Holocaust Remembrance Center in Jerusalem. Her most recent work has become a joyful celebration of life, and can be seen at: https://www.miriambrysk.com

When Miriam was in her mid-70s, she began to write about her Holocaust experiences, and I was honored to be her editor. Her award-winning memoir, *Amidst the Shadows of Trees—A Holocaust Child's Survival in the Partisans,* published in 2013, was followed by: *The Scroll of Remembrance: Jewish Communities Destroyed in the Shoah* (2013); *The Stones Weep: Teaching the Holocaust through a Survivor's Art*, written with Margaret G. Lincoln, Ph.D. (Winner of the Independent Publishers of New England 2014 Book of the Year Award), and a poetry collection: *Etched in My Memory: Refections of a Holocaust Survivor* (2015).

When I became Miriam's editor in 2012, we were total strangers, living in different states, and communicating only by phone and by email. We didn't meet until after the first book we worked on was published, and I was overjoyed to visit her and Henry in Ann Arbor. At this time, I was also working on my own book, *WOMEN OF VALOR: Polish Jewish Resisters to the Third Reich.* From our first conversation, I realized that along with Manya Feldman, Faye Schulman, and Lola Lieber, Miriam Brysk was indeed a Woman of Valor, and should have a chapter in my book. Fortunately, she accepted my invitation— and the story of this spunky little girl is always the highlight of my speaking engagements. Our professional relationship quickly evolved into a treasured, once-in-a lifetime friendship. Writing *Victory* together has been a labor of love—for each other, for our lost relatives, for all who have been touched by the Holocaust, and for our readers. We are both grateful to be able to share Miriam's story with you, and we welcome your comments and suggestions.

You can keep up with our various projects by going to our websites:

https://www.avictoryformiriam.com
https://www.miriambrysk.com
https://www.joannedgilbert.com
https://www.women-of-valor.org
https://www.facebook.com/JoanneDGilbertAuthor/

Acknowledgements

Miriam and I are grateful to our beloved family, friends, and readers who encouraged us to write, *A Victory for Miriam! The Little Jewish Girl Who Defied the Nazis*. We also thank our wonderful proof-readers, Laura Engle Sahr, Susan Dubin, Sara Melvin, Sharon Singer, Bobbie Best, Berna Heyman, and Dr. Regina Lederman, as well as my granddaughter, Julia Grace Gilbert, and my brother, Gary Ron, for their meticulous attention to detail, invaluable feedback, and unfailing belief in this book.

There would be no book without the magic of our kind and highly-skilled art and technical professionals, who all went above and beyond the call of duty to create a beautiful book: Illustrator Angel Luna's (www.angellluna. com) prodigious artistic talent, understanding, and commitment are evident in each of his brilliant sketches, including the little girl on the cover. Lisa Frederickson (www.focus7publishing.com) never fails to provide the support we need—from websites to Ebooks, to moral support. Anya Wilcox, (www. designintersection.com) listened with her heart to our request to implement my granddaughter, Julia Gilbert's cover concept, and then implemented it beautifully. The book's interior designer, Tamian Wood (www.beyonddesign-international.com), graciously met every challenge, and patiently put all the pieces together. Special thanks go to Reese Melvin, Madelyn Moss, and Alana Luna for being models for the front cover. We are grateful to everyone who joined us in honoring Miriam, and ensuring that her legacy will continue to inspire others.

GLOSSARY

1. *Aktions*: A German word meaning organized violent attacks on Jewish communities that often included deportations to concentration and death camps.

2. **Allied Forces of World War I:** Included Great Britain, France, Russia, Italy and the United States.

3. **Allied Forces of World War II:** Included Great Britain, the Soviet Union, France and the United States.

4. *Anschluss*: A German word meaning political unification—the bringing together of two countries. This described the German's annexation of Austria in March 1938.

5. **Antisemitism:** Hatred of Jewish people.

6. **Axis Powers of World War II:** Included Germany, Italy, Japan.

7. **Belarus:** The current country of Belarus, once also known as White Russia, was part of the Soviet Union until the Germans broke the Molotov-Ribbentrop Pact in June 1941, and occupied it. When the war ended, Belarus again came under Soviet control until it became an independent country in 1991.

8. **Bielski Brothers:** These brothers grew up in the village of Nowogródek, near Lida. They escaped their ghetto and formed a highly effective partisan group in the forest. The 2008 award-winning movie, "Defiance," which was based on Nechama Tec's 1993 book, Defiance: The Bielski Partisans, tells the story of these heroes.

9. **Blitzkrieg (Blitz):** This is the German word for "Lightning War." It is a fast, deadly, military attack from the air and land, that catches the victims unprepared, and usually results in a fast victory.

10. *Bocci Ball*: An outdoor game similar to bowling, that is very popular in Italy.

11. **British Army's Jewish Brigade:** The British Army's Jewish Brigade Group was created in September 1944. More than 5,000 Jewish volunteers from

Palestine fought against the Germans in Italy from March 1945 until the war ended in May 1945. After the war, the Brigade created displaced persons camps for survivors, and helped Jewish refugees emigrate—against Britain's orders—from Eastern Europe into Palestine. For more information, go to: https://encyclopedia.ushmm.org/content/en/article/jewish-brigade-group

12. *Cadre*: A small group of people working to achieve a specific goal.

13. **Casualty:** A person who has been injured or killed as a result of an accident, a crime, or war.

14. **Censored:** When written communication is erased, redacted, or otherwise eliminated by the government, it is said to have been "censored."

15. **Central Powers of World War I:** These included Germany, Austria-Hungary, Ottoman Empire and Bulgaria.

16. *Ciocia*: The Polish word for "Aunt."

17. **Collaborator:** A person who helps his country's enemy.

18. **Customs:** A section of a government building at a port where officials determine if incoming passengers can be admitted to the country.

19. **DDT:** A chemical compound that not only kills insects and lice, but as we learned years later, is also dangerous for the environment—as well as humans. It was banned in the US in 1972.

20. *Der Führer*: Adolf Hitler gave himself the title, *"der Führer,"* meaning the highest leader in the German government during the Third Reich.

21. *Exodus*: As recounted in the Old Testament's Exodus, Passover (Pesach) is a Jewish holiday celebrating the Jews' escape or "exodus," from Egypt

22. **Gas gangrene:** A bacterial infection which causes body tissue to decay and die.

23. **Gentile:** A person who is not Jewish.

24. *Gestapo*: The abbreviation for the *Geheime Staatspolizei,* the secret police of Nazi Germany and German-occupied Europe. ***Stormtroopers*** were Hitler's merciless, semi-military group.

25. ***Ghetto***: The word,"ghetto," is thought to have originated in Venice, Italy in the early 1500s. The city leaders decided that Jews should be required to live in a small, filthy area on one of Venice's islands. They called it the "Ghetto Nuova." The word, "ghetto," has several possible meanings, but in this case, it refers to the area or street where Jews are forced to live. "Nuova" means "new."

26. ***Gondolas***: Traditional, flat-bottomed Venetian rowboats. ***Vaporetti*** are motorized water-buses.

27. **Greenhorns:** This is an insult often used to describe refugees who have come to the United States.

28. ***Handverkshtaten***: These small factories, sometimes outside of the ghetto, provided employment and a small degree of safety, for skilled Jewish workers and artisans who were considered "valuable" to the Germans.

29. **Hernia:** This medical condition happens when there is a weakness or hole in a muscle wall, allowing the intestine to poke through.

30. **Holocaust:** (From the Greek: *Holos*=all, *kaustos*=burnt) Also known as the *Shoah* (Hebrew: *catastrophe*), the Holocaust was the period of time between 1933 and 1945 when Germany's Third Reich government, under the leadership of Adolf Hitler, murdered over six-million Jews in their campaign to eliminate the Jews of Europe. A "Holocaust survivor" is someone who lived through this terrible experience.

31. ***Horah:*** The Horah is a Jewish circle dance often accompanied by the tune, Hava Nagila, which means, Let Us Rejoice! It is traditionally danced at Jewish weddings and other joyous occasions.

32. ***Judenfrei***: This German word means that a place has been made completely free of Jews by starving, deporting, or murdering them.

33. ***Judenrat***: A group of Jews organized in the ghettos by the Nazis to carry out their orders.

34. ***Kibbutzim***: The people who live and work communally on a farm in Israel called a kibbutz.

35. ***Kristallnacht***: A German word meaning "the night of broken glass." This was a systematic deadly attack against Jews across Germany and Austria on

November 9-10, 1938. Synagogues, Jewish-owned businesses, and homes were vandalized, destroyed and looted. Approximately 35,000 Jewish men were seized and sent to concentration camps.

36. **Lida:** The city in Poland where Miriam's father had grown up. When Miriam's family fled from Warsaw, they went to Lida, because until June 1941, when the Germans occupied Warsaw, Lida was controlled by the Soviet Union.

37. *Mamaloshen*: A Yiddish word meaning the "mother tongue," or first language of the Jewish people.

38. **Molotov-Ribbentrop Non-Aggression Pact:** Signed on August 23, 1939, this agreement which divided Poland between Germany and the USSR, was a promise that Germany and the USSR would not attack each other. This Agreement remained in effect until the Germans broke it by attacking the Soviet Union on June 22, 1941.

39. **Mourners'** *Kaddish:* Jewish prayer for the dead.

40. *Nazi*: A member of Hitler's National Socialist German Workers' Party.

41. ***Orden Lenina***: The prestigious Order of Lenin was the highest civilian award given by the Soviet government.

42. **Partisans:** Illegal, secret, armed freedom fighters who fought against the Nazis.

43. **Passover:** This Jewish holiday (known as *Pesach* in Hebrew), celebrates Jewish liberation from slavery in Egypt

44. **Polio:** Also known as poliomyelitis or infantile paralysis, this highly contagious virus usually begins with chills and fever, progresses to muscle pains, breathing difficulty, then paralysis, and often, death. Its victims were mostly young children. This terrible disease has been almost 100% eliminated because of the Salk Vaccine invented by Jonas Salk in the early 1950s.

45. ***Rabbi***: A Jewish scholar who is appointed to be a religious leader. A ***cantor*** leads the singing portions of Jewish services.

46. **Relief agencies:** Organizations that help Jews who are in desperate need. One of these was *Bricha*, which helped Jewish refugees get to Palestine,

ended when Israel declared its independence in 1948. The largest and most well-known relief agency is the American Jewish Joint Distribution Committee (often called, the "JOINT"), which was founded in 1914, and continues to this day. It provided money to help Jews escape the Nazis during the war, and then to find safe housing after the war.

47. **Refugee:** A person who has been forced to escape from his or her homeland because of persecution, violence, war, or natural disaster.

48. **Refugee camps:** Were set up by organizations and governments to temporarily house refugees. Sometimes these were actual camps with tents, other times they were hotels, apartments, churches and hospitals.

49. *Rosh Hashanah*: This autumn Jewish Holiday is the first of the 10-day Jewish High Holy Days celebrating the New Year. The final day is *Yom Kippur*, the Day of Penitence, when Jews ask forgiveness from those they have hurt or offended.

50. *Seder*: This ceremonial Jewish feast celebrates the beginning of Passover. Part of the ceremony is the reading of the *Haggadah*—which recounts the story of the Jews escape. Also included are special foods, songs, and the drinking of wine

51. *Shabbat*: This is the Jewish ceremonial meal served at sundown on Friday night, to mark the beginning of the Sabbath—Saturday—the Jewish day of rest.

52. **Soviet Union/USSR/Russia:** In 1918, following the Russian Revolution, and World War I, the country of Russia became known as Soviet Republic. In 1922, a new government was formed, the Union of the Soviet Socialist Republics, which remained in power until 1991, when the country became known as Russia again.

53. **Spam:** Processed, cooked, and canned, pork that was used by the military during World War II because it was convenient and easy to carry.

54. **Star of David:** Also known as the *Magen David*, this 6-point star symbolizes the Jewish people.

✡

55. *Swastika*: Originally a Sanskrit word meaning "good luck," This is an ancient cross symbol whose 4 arms are bent in right angles, which became the symbol of the German Nazi party.

56. **Tenements:** Inhabited by very poor people, these narrow, over-crowded, apartment buildings, had few windows and poor ventilation.

57. **Third Reich:** The name of Adolf Hitler's German government. *Reich* means "empire." There had been two previous German Empires.

58. *Tikkun Olam*: This Hebrew phrase means to "repair" or "heal" the world.

59. *Torah*: According to the Jewish religion, the *Torah* contains the laws of God as were told to Moses, and then written down in the first five books of the Hebrew Bible, also know as the Old Testament.

60. **Versailles Treaty:** World War I came to an end on November 11, 1918, when Germany surrendered. Of the 19 peace agreements that were signed, the *Treaty of Versailles* (June 28, 1919) was the most important. It was signed by the *Allied Forces*, including Britain, France, Russia, Italy, the United States, and the Central Powers including: Germany (under protest), Austria-Hungary, Ottoman Empire and Bulgaria.

61. **Visa:** A government document that allows a person to legally enter a foreign country.

62. **Warsaw:** Capital of Poland.

63. **Whooping Cough:** A highly contagious disease that causes victims to cough violently. These coughs have a high-pitched whooping sound.

64. **Yiddish:** (*Mamaloshen*)A language used by Jews from central and eastern Europe. It is derived from German, and includes words from Hebrew as well as other languages in the various regions where Jews live.

65. *Zemlyanka:* A camouflaged, underground bunker in the forest where Jews hid from the Germans

A Victory for Miriam! Classroom Activities
by Sara Melvin and Joanne Gilbert

Here are some discussion/journal questions and classroom activity ideas for individuals, partners, small groups, and/or the whole class, that will allow students to explore the topics in *Victory*, and demonstrate proficiency in vocabulary, reading comprehension, text interpretation, and oral presentations.

Pre-Reading:

1. What do you already know about the Holocaust?

2. How old were you, and under what circumstances did you first learn about the Holocaust?

3. How did learning about the Holocaust affect you?

4. Who were the first Holocaust victims you learned about?

5. How would you explain the Holocaust to someone who has never heard of it?

6. Why do some people deny that the Holocaust took place? How does this make you feel? Have you ever met a "Holocaust Denier"? If yes, how did you respond to his/her denial?

7. Why is it important to document the personal stories of Holocaust victims?

8. Based on the book's title, what do you think Miriam's victory will be?

9. Discuss and give examples of the meaning of the following words: victory, personal victory, family victory, social victory.

10. Describe a victory from your life.

11. Why do you think the Holocaust happened?

12. What are some ways people can try to prevent a Holocaust from happening again?

Note to Readers:

1. The word "Holocaust" is introduced, and defined. Research this word and draw a picture or write a poem that expresses both the literal and figurative meaning of "Holocaust."

Prologue:

1. Discuss the purpose of the Prologue. Does it make you want to read more? Why/why not? What questions does the Prologue bring up for you?

2. Write a short story about an event in your early life, using the Prologue/Flashback technique.

3. In the Prologue, the word "refugees" is introduced, and defined. Explore the etymology (history) of the word "refugees," and create a timeline or storyboard tracing its development to today's use of the word.

4. What do you know about refugees in the world today?

Chapter 1: *Early Childhood/Warsaw*

1. Have students write poems describing the bombing in Warsaw from either a child's or adult's point of view. Poems should focus on the sounds, sights, smells, tastes, and emotions that would have been experienced during this time.

2. In Chapter 1, Miriam learns what the word, "war," means. Create 5 sentences that include metaphors or similes for the word "war." Use the sentences as captions for drawings you create to show the literal and metaphorical meanings of "war."

Chapter 2: *The Lida Ghetto*

1. How did Miriam's life in the Lida Ghetto differ from her early life in Warsaw?

2. Discuss how it feels to move to a new home. Discuss what it would be like if the new home was horrible.

3. Write a Journal from the German officer's point of view on the day he picked Miriam up and held her. What would have happened next if he had know she was Jewish?

Chapter 3: *Life in the Lida Ghetto*

"Living so close to death made dying just a part of living."

1. Discuss the meaning of this quotation in relation to Miriam's experiences. In what ways can horrific circumstances become routine parts of every day life?

2. Ask students to draw pictures, write poems, newspaper articles, or a series of text/tweet exchanges based on this quotation.

Chapter 4: *A Surprise Sanctuary*

1. Discuss taking risks to help others in need. Have students taken a risk to help others? Have they been in a position where someone took a risk to help them? Under what circumstances would someone choose to ignore someone instead of helping him/her?

2. Have students write a letter either asking someone for help, or a "Thank You" letter to someone who took a risk to help them.

3. Discuss the risk Ciocia put herself and her daughter in by keeping Miriam.

4. Ask students to write either a "Thank You" letter from Miriam to Ciocia, or from Miriam's mother to Ciocia.

Chapter 5: *Escaping the Lida ghetto*

1. Discussion: What are civilian rebellions? What causes them? Where/when have they taken place in history? Are they taking place today? Compare/contrast civilian rebellions of the past with those of the present day.

2. Class discussion/journals: If you'd been a Jewish teenager living in the Lida ghetto, would you join the Jewish Partisans? Why/Why not?

3. Write a journal from Mama's point of view about the difficult decision to leave the Lida ghetto and join the partisans. Describe how she convinced Papa that they all needed to go.

Chapter 6: *The Jewish Partisans*

1. Discuss how the following passage shows Miriam's pride in the partisans, and how it affects her own self-esteem: *"What a comfort and joy it was to be surrounded by Jews who were capable, healthy, and proud. They were not cowering slaves who worked for merciless masters. They were not brutalized victims dying painfully in a ghetto. These powerful Jews worked together to save Jewish lives. And they worked together to destroy Germans. I could feel the strength, the pride, the skill, and determination of these unbowed Jews,*

and for the first —but definitely not the last —time in my life, an energizing wave of Jewish pride surged within me."

2. Ask students to draw a picture, write a poem, a letter to a friend, a news article, a series of texts/tweets based on the passage.

Chapter 7: *The Soviet Partisans*

1. Discuss the ways in which Miriam's mother was a powerful force in Miriam's life. How would Mama's life have been different if she had not been a mother?

2. Ask students to create a representation of Mama's importance. It can be a drawing, a collage, a poem, or a song.

3. Discuss the reasons why the Soviet Partisans would not take a child.

4. Have students write a journal entry from the point of view of a Soviet partisan who had refused to take a child along with his group in the forest.

Chapter 8: *The Forest Hospital*

1. In what ways did Miriam change in this chapter? What was the reason for the change? How does she feel about this transformation? How does it affect her behavior?

2. Discuss the ways people present themselves to others. Why is it sometimes necessary to wear a "false front"?

3. Journal: Have you ever had to put on a "false front"?

Chapter 9: *Liberated but Not Free*

1. Discussion/Journals: Have you ever had to adjust to a big disappointment in your life?

2. Create a storyboard or illustrated timeline showing how Miriam's life has changed since Chapter 1.

Chapter 10: *Lublin and First Love*

1. Class Discussion: What are the effects of overcrowding in classrooms? Discuss the challenges of so many people living in one big room.

2. Journal: Write about a time you had to function in an overcrowded situation.

3. Write a journal from Miriam's father's point of view about his daughter's new relationship with the boy.

4. Create a dialogue between Miriam's parents about their different impression of Miriam's relationship with this boy.

5. What are Mama's strengths? Her challenges? What personality traits does she possess that help her survive?

6. Write a journal entry from Mama's point of view about the mental, physical, and emotional challenges she faces every day.

7. Journal: Have you ever had to put aside your own needs in order to protect another person?

Chapter 11: *Leaving Poland—Again!*

1. What are the Brysks grateful for in this chapter? What heartbreak do they endure in the midst of their safety?

2. Describe Turda. How does life in Turda compare/contrast with living in the forest? How does it compare with the horror that was still raging in western Poland?

3. List all the reasons Miriam feels gratitude for her life Turda.

4. Journal: What are you grateful for?

Chapter 12: *Wandering Jews*

"So, yes, freedom—whatever that meant—was a great relief, but what good was freedom if we were still powerless over our own lives, and couldn't even imagine a future?"

1. Discuss the meaning of this quote

2. Write an essay showing the irony that the Jews had been liberated but were not welcome in so many countries. Use examples from the book to support your thesis.

3. Write an essay showing the irony of the Jews being liberated by, and then totally controlled by the Soviets. Use examples from the book.

4. Research *Bricha* and create a presentation explaining what it was and its importance in saving Jewish refugees.

Chapter 13: *A Surprise Reunion*

1. Why was the Shabbat service so heart-wrenching for Miriam and her mother? How does the beauty of the synagogue contrast with the ugliness of Miriam's memories?

2. Write a poem or a dramatic scene in which the physical setting is a stark contrast to the emotions of the characters in it.

3. From Mama's point of view, write a letter to her American uncles asking for their help in sponsoring the family's immigration to the United States. Explain the family's current circumstances and the urgency of their need physical, mental and emotional needs to emigrate to the US.

Chapter 14: *Hellos and Goodbyes in Italy*

1. Discuss the difference between "sympathy" and "empathy." Which emotion do students feel for Miriam?

2. Write a letter of *sympathy* to Miriam. Include lines from a poem of encouragement that you have researched.

3. Write a letter of *empathy* to Miriam. Include an example from you own life that shows you understand her feelings.

Chapter 15: *Big Changes*

"I felt as if I were wriggling out of a scratchy, too small, pain-filled cocoon, and I was more than ready to fly."

1. Discuss the meaning of this quote and ask students when they might have felt this way.

2. Create an artistic image that reflects the meaning of this quote.

3. Create an acrostic poem that spells "BUTTERFLY" inspired by the recent changes in Miriam's life.

Chapter 16: *Greenhorns in the Golden Land*

1. Why does Miriam have such mixed feelings about her American family?

2. Journal: Write about a time when you had mixed feelings about a relative.

3. Role-Play a scene between Miriam, her American relatives, and a therapist who tries to get them to see each other's reality.

4. Create a monologue for Miriam in which she tells her American relatives how she feels about them, and what she really needs from them.

Chapter 17: *School Daze*

1. A new school year can be very stressful. What stress does Miriam experience at the beginning of this school year? In what ways is she more confident than in the previous school year?

2. Write a diary entry about the first day of your own new school year.

3. Create a diary entry from Miriam about her experiences in this chapter. Include observations about school, family, parents, home and emotions.

4. Discuss why people ignore other people. What does being ignored feel like? Why did the other students ignore Miriam?

5. Write a journal about a time you were ignored or ignored someone else.

Chapter 18: *A Victory for Miriam!*

1. How many victories did Miriam experience?

2. Why do you think she was able to succeed in spite of the horrors she had experienced?

3. In a small group or as a class, brainstorm 10 questions to ask Miriam in an interview. Include "open-ended" questions.

Epilogue:

1. Why is it important for Holocaust survivors to tell the stories of their experiences?

2. Write a letter from present-day Miriam to her parents explaining why she decided to write this book.

POST-READING:

Discussion/Essay/Speech Topics

1. What was the Holocaust? Why did it happen? Could it happen again?

2. Explain the differences between being a victim, a perpetrator, and a bystander.

3. Compare/Contrast Miriam's life with that of a typical American child.

4. Discuss how children today who live in desperate circumstances are similar or different from Miriam.

5. Why would a little girl want to be a boy? Explain the various circumstances that caused Miriam's feelings about being a girl to change.

6. Take a side either FOR or AGAINST joining the partisans in the Lida ghetto. Use evidence from the chapter to support your choice.

7. Persuade a friend/sibling to leave the ghetto and join the partisans.

8. Persuade a friend/sibling to stay in the ghetto instead of joining the partisans.

9. Discuss the importance of the Jewish religion in Miriam's life. Give examples from the book.

10. Discuss the importance of the various physical settings in *Victory*. Include examples of how Miriam is affected by her surroundings.

11. Explain what you think is the overall theme of Miriam's life. Use examples from the book to support your thesis.

12. Discuss why you think Miriam survived the Holocaust. Provide evidence from the book to support your thesis.

13. Discuss how Miriam's experiences in the Holocaust helped and/or hurt her ability to adjust to life in the US.

14. What is "evil"? Is it inborn or learned? Can normal people commit evil acts? Can evil people change?

Create and Enact Dramatic Scenes:

1. Choose a scene from the book, and expand upon it or provide dialogue. Then rewrite the scene with a different ending.

2. Select a scene and update it to modern day life.

3. Write a scene of a play based on the daily activities within a partisan camp.

4. Write a scene of a play based on the daily activities in a German military camp.

5. Write a scene, set in Miriam's Brooklyn school, in which she tries to explain the Holocaust to another student. Show how the other students react.

6. Write a scene in which it is "Show and Tell Day" at Miriam's school. The other students bring in favorite toys, interesting mechanical devices, and souvenirs from vacations. Miriam brings in a ragged, dirty, yellow Star of David that had once been attached to her clothing.

EXTENDED ACTIVITIES

1. Using historically accurate information, create a newspaper based on one day in Miriam's life in the partisans. Include an editorial page, an editorial cartoon, an advice column, want-ads, sports, social events, local, Polish, and international news.

2. Create a video game based on Miriam's experiences during the Holocaust.

3. Create a Survival Manual for new partisans. Be sure to include tips for crossing a swamp on slippery logs, while carrying an injured comrade.

4. Create a presentation showing the challenges that confronted the partisans and the methods they used to deal with these challenges.

5. Create an interactive map showing Miriam's journey, and the major events that took place along the way.

6. Analyze artist Angel L. Luna's style and create images from *Victory* in the styles of other artists such as: Picasso, Monet, Van Gogh.

7. What kind of job would Dr. Miasnik be qualified to do when he first arrived in the US? Create a resume for Dr. Chaim Miasnik to present at his first job interview in Brooklyn.

8. Create a skit in which you are a prospective employer interviewing Dr. Miasnik for a job in the US.

9. Choose 20+ Vocabulary words from *Victory,* and write an historically accurate short story using these words—or their forms—correctly.

10. Create a booklet of word games using the vocabulary words in *Victory.*

11. Create a Quiz Show, where teams compete for the correct answers based on information from *Victory.*

12. Create a presentation about the Holocaust geared for younger students.

13. Contact your local Jewish Community Center, synagogue, or Jewish Federation to arrange for a Holocaust survivor to come to your class.

14. Contact the authors to speak at your school or to arrange a Skype book-talk with the class. info@joannedgilbert.com

I created this collage in 2006 by combining 2 images that show different aspects of my father's life. The right side of Papa's face comes from a photo taken in 1942 in the Lida ghetto. The left side of his face is from an photo taken in 1945, in a displaced persons' camp in Turda, Romania.

Gallery

In Memory of Papa

From *"Refugees on Rosh Hashanah"*

. . . Rosh Hashanah—Jewish New Year 1946
Was the first holiday observance since before the war
As we lost most of our families in the Shoah
We had no rabbi
We had no cantor
But we had my father, the scholar and surgeon . . .
with his beautiful voice . . .
he led the entire service
in the dining room of our compound
Many of us were overcome with tears . . .
To witness refugees huddled together
Praying to a God we thought had abandoned us

In Memory of Aunt Ala

From: *"A Ring of Love"*

You left us for Warsaw that fall
To care for your elderly parents
We pleaded: "We have suffered so much together,
Don't leave us now, please don't go."
You left me your ruby ring . . .
meant for me to wear if I survived the war . . .

My Granddaughter Sarah is named after you . . .
our eyes cloud over when we speak of you
In those tears, an eternal bond of memory and love
Shortly, I'll pass the ruby ring—and your love—on to her

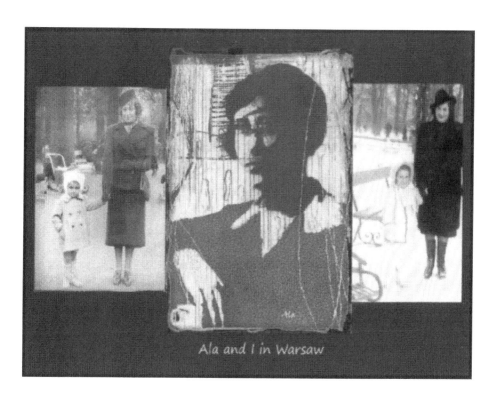

Ala and I in Warsaw

I created this collage in 2006 using 3 old photos of my Aunt Ala in Warsaw. It shows how close we were. The center image shows Ala as a teenager. On the left, she and I walk in the park in autumn, 1937. On the right, we walk through the same park in winter 1938.

My grandmother Chana Liba and I

I made this collage in 2006 using old photos of my Grandmother, Chana Liba. The image of her face in the upper left hand corner was taken at my father's medical school graduation. The center image shows us walking in a Warsaw park in summer 1939, just before the war broke out. The image along the bottom is of Warsaw Jews being deported to Treblinka.

In Memory of My Grandmother Chana Liba

From: *"No Time for Silence"*

Their faces haunt my memory
Hearts constricted in terror
To suffer and endure
Shoulders curved
Heads drooped
Anguished outcries
Final prayers
Silence

In Memory of My Mother, Bronka Miasnik

From *"Hand in Hand"*

Shadows of leaves flickering in the moonlight
Desperate voices lost in total darkness
Sounds of snow crushing beneath our feet
Panic consuming our frozen bodies . . .
I cling to her, my mantle of protection
I am cold and hungry, Mama
Be still Mirele, we have to run my child . . .

I made this collage of my mother and me in 2006. I used a photo taken just after Liberation in 1945, and incorporated images of our lost family. It shows how our past and our loved ones run through, and connect our hearts and souls.

From: *"A Rose by Any Name"* —by Judy Brysk

1957

As an infant, you were my "Mama."
The relationship was pure and simple.
You loved and fed me.
You were the center of my life.
The smile that meant the most was your smile.
Being held by you was the safest place in my world . . .

Now as you are growing older,
you are again becoming my "Mama".
I want to lift the burdens of the world
and make your life easier . . .
I want you to feel that being in my arms
is the safest place in the world.

2013

From: *"My Mom"* —by Havi Brysk Mandell

1959

My mother is a dervishly dancing phoenix
Re-birthed from the ashes
With the fire of a passion to be
Her own unique presence
A Maverick. Individualist. Powerhouse.
Always different and proud of it:
She sees things as no one else does
Brings disparate things together into new wholes . . .

Always leaving a profound mark wherever she goes.
She is a scientist, exploring and experimenting
With relentless curiosity and the heart of an artist.
artist and poet, pouring feeling into creative form
With a scientist's questioning mind.
She is a Survivor, not a label, but a responsibility
To speak for those who no longer can
To remember them and honor them.

2015

Original Art by Angel L. Luna

The story of Miriam Brysk's childhood during the Holocaust immediately drew me into her life and touched my heart. I was also very moved by the powerful Holocaust art she created later in life. I am so privileged to have been able to create the original art included in this very special book.

As I thought about what Miriam was experiencing, thinking, and feeling during her traumatic childhood, I realized how important it was for my artwork to not just be illustrations, but to actually represent her experiences while echoing her thoughts and feelings. I thought about what a little girl on the run for her life in the woods and swamps would use if she got the chance to make art. Since I wanted my work to honor what hers might have been, I used simple tools: wood sticks that I found outside, Indian ink, paper tissue for texture, cardboard for scraping and moving the ink and water on 5X7" clay-board panels.

I hope the resulting images honor this remarkable story, and inspire readers to make their own art in honor of little Miriam Brysk.

— Angel L. Luna

A Surprise During the Blitz

A Zemlyanka in the Snow

Papa and Patient in Forest Hospital

Desperate Passengers

SS Marine Falcon

ABOUT THE AUTHORS

Miriam M. Brysk, Ph.D   Joanne D. Gilbert, M. Ed

Miriam M. Brysk, Ph.D, is a child Holocaust survivor who was born in Warsaw, Poland, and currently resides in Ann Arbor, Michigan. After the Blitzkreig, she and her parents fled Warsaw, going to Soviet-controlled Lida, in what is now Belarus, where they were eventually interned in the Lida ghetto. After managing to survive the horrific Lida Massacre, they escaped to the forest, where they lived with partisans for 18 months. After the liberation, Miriam and her parents emigrated to the United States in 1947, and settled in Brooklyn. Having had only a few months of schooling, Miriam went on to earn a Master of Science in Bacteriology from the University of Michigan, then a doctorate in Biological Sciences from Columbia University, and became a respected scientist. Upon her retirement in 2000, Miriam became an artist, author, and public speaker, whose work focuses on the Holocaust. Her three major art exhibits, "In a Confined Silence," "Children of the Holocaust," and "Scroll of Remembrance," have received outstanding reviews in over 38 exhibitions. Three of her works are part of the permanent art collection at the Yad Vashem World Holocaust Remembrance Center in Jerusalem. Miriam's award-winning memoir, Amidst the Shadows of Trees: A Holocaust Child's Survival in the Partisans, was published in 2013. Her art book, Scroll of Remembrance: Jewish Communities Destroyed in the Shoah, was published in 2013. Her third book, award-winning The Stones Weep: Teaching the Holocaust through a Survivor's Art, written in conjunction with Margaret G. Lincoln, Ph.D, was published in 2014. Her book of poetry, Etched in My Memory: Reflections of a Holocaust Survivor, was published in 2015. For more information, and to hear an oral interview with Miriam, go to: https://holocaust.umd.umich.edu/brysk/

Joanne D. Gilbert, M. Ed, was born in Detroit, Michigan, and relocated to the San Francisco Bay Area in 1985. She has resided in Las Vegas, Nevada since 2004. As a post-World War II Baby Boomer, growing up in Oak Park, Michigan, a predominantly Jewish suburb of Detroit, Joanne's childhood was profoundly influenced by stories of the Holocaust. As the great-granddaughter of Holocaust victims, Joanne grew up listening to her grandmother, Millie Ron's stories of the family and friends who were murdered in the liquidation of the Vilna ghetto. These influences are the foundation of Joanne's dedication to Holocaust education. Her specific focus is documenting and celebrating the Jewish and Gentile men, women, and children who successfully defied the Nazis, and went on to live long, loving and productive lives. Her first book, award-winning, WOMEN OF VALOR: Polish Jewish Resisters to the Third Reich, was published in 2014. An updated, revised edition was published in 2018, and includes a chapter about Miriam Brysk.

Upon retiring from more than forty years as an educator, Joanne founded her own personal historian business, "YOUR WRITE TIME! Personal History Products & Services," through which she helps clients create engaging and informative memoirs. Joanne is also an editor, and has worked on eight Holocaust-related memoirs, including Miriam Brysk's Among the Shadows of Trees. Joanne has travelled extensively throughout the Untied States, Canada, and Europe, doing research, conducting interviews, and making presentations about the remarkable men and women who successfully defied the Nazis. In 2018, she was honored to make a presentation at the Vilna Jewish Library in Vilnius, Lithuania. This was a profoundly gratifying experience because her ancestors had lived in Vilna for generations before being murdered by the Nazis.

In addition to speaking at schools, churches, synagogues, libraries, book clubs, and community organizations, Joanne's recent presentations include the Warsaw, Poland Jewish Community Center, the International Association of Jewish Genealogy Associations Annual Conferences in Salt Lake City, Seattle, and Warsaw, and the Freya von Moltke International Institute for Peace in Kreisau, Poland. In conjunction with the Las Vegas Sperling Kronberg Mack Holocaust Resource Center, Joanne conducts popular workshops for teachers who plan to incorporate Holocaust education in their curricula.

Joanne welcomes comments from her readers and audiences, as well as opportunities to make presentations about "Resistance & Remembrance: Celebrating the Heroes and Heroines of the Shoah"; "Daffodil Day: Commemorating the Warsaw Ghetto Uprising"; "Recovering the Lost Mezuzahs of Poland"; as well as Memoir Writing Workshops.

For more information about Joanne, please contact her at:
info@joannedgilbert.com,
or go to: www.joannedgilbert.com,
www.women-of-valor.org,
www.avictoryforMiriam.com
and visit her Facebook Page:
https://www.facebook.com/JoanneDGilbertAuthor/

SELECTED RESOURCES

Images: Unless otherwise noted, photos and collages are courtesy of the Miriam M. Brysk collection.

Photo on pages 1, 137: Courtesy of Alex Gilbert: 2019
Photos on pages 111, 112, 129 from www.depositphotos.com

Maps: Created by Lisa Frederickson, www.focus7consulting.com

Websites:
Jewish Virtual Library: https:/www.jewishvirtuallibrary.org
https://www.joannedgilbert.com
Lida Memorial Foundation: https://www.lidaholocaustfoundation.org
https://www.miriambrysk.com
USHMM: https://www.ushmm.org
https://www.women-of-valor.org
Yad Vashem: https://www.yadvashem.org

Made in the USA
Lexington, KY
04 December 2019